ONE WEEK LOAN

MANCHESTER
UNIVERSITY PRESS

Politics Today
Series Editor: Bill Jones

Italian politics today

Hilary Partridge

Manchester University Press

Manchester and New York

Distributed exclusively in the USA by St. Martin's Press

Published by Manchester University Press
Oxford Road, Manchester M13 9NR, UK
and Room 400, 175 Fifth Avenue, New York, NY 10010, USA

Distributed exclusively in the USA by
St. Martin's Press, Inc., 175 Fifth Avenue, New York,
NY 10010, USA

Distributed exclusively in Canada by
UBC Press, University of British Columbia, 6344 Memorial Road,
Vancouver, BC, Canada V6T 1Z2

British Library Cataloguing-in-Publication Data
A catalogue record for this book is available from the British Library

Library of Congress Cataloging-in-Publication Data
Partridge, Hilary.
    Italian politics today / Hilary Partridge.
      p. cm. – (Politics today)
    Includes bibliographical references (p. 196) and index.
    ISBN 0-7190-4943-1 (hardback). – ISBN 0-7190-4944-X (paperback)
    1. Italy—Politics and government—1976–1994.   2. Italy—Politics
and government—1994–.   I. Title.   II. Series: Politics today
(Manchester, England)
JN5451.P365   1998
320.945'.09'045–dc21   98-7197

ISBN   0 7190 4943 1 *hardback*
         0 7190 4944 X *paperback*

First published 1998

05 04 03 02 01 00   10 9 8 7 6 5 4 3 2

Typeset by Ralph Footring, Derby
Printed by Bell & Bain Ltd, Glasgow

Contents

Preface

Italy has long been stereotyped as a nation of upheaval and chaos, in which weak and incompetent political leaderships govern precariously in the face of an anarchic society. But the surface turmoil of Italian politics long masked a changeless hierarchical order. The Christian Democrats and their allies were allowed to rule undisturbed because the only alternative was government by the Communists. In the early 1990s, the 'regime of the parties' that had ruled Italy since the end of the Second World War collapsed under the accumulated costs of holding on to power. In 1996, the Communists' successors, who no longer appeared as a threat after the demise of the Communist regimes in Europe, took power as the leaders of a new alliance of progressive parties.

In Giuseppe di Lampedusa's novel *The Leopard*, set in the turmoil of unification, the Prince understands that things can stay as they are so long as they appear to change. This book is motivated by the efforts of my good friends in Italy, and many like them, who continue to fight for a real change for the better.

Abbreviations

ACLI	Associazione Cristiana dei Lavoratori Italiani (Christian Associations of Italian Workers)
AN	Alleanza Nazionale (National Alliance)
BR	Brigate Rosse (Red Brigades)
CGIL	Confederazione Generale Italiana del Lavoro (Italian General Confederation of Labour)
CISL	Confederazione Italiana Sindacati Lavoratori (Italian Confederation of Workers' Unions)
CLNs	*comitati di liberazione nazionale* (committees of national liberation)
DC	Democrazia Cristiana (Christian Democrats)
EMU	Economic and Monetary Union
INPS	Istituto Nazionale di Previdenza Sociale (National Institute for Social Insurance)
IRI	Istituto per la Ricostruzione Industriale (Institute for Industrial Reconstruction)
MPs	members of parliament
MSI	Movimento Sociale Italiano (Italian Social Movement)
PCI	Partito Comunista Italiano (Italian Communist Party)
PDS	Partito Democratico di Sinistra (Democratic Party of the Left)
PLI	Partito Liberale Italiano (Italian Liberal Party)
PPI	Partito Popolare Italiano (Italian Popular Party)
PR	proportional representation
PRI	Partito Repubblicano Italiano (Italian Republican Party)
PSI	Partito Socialista Italiano (Italian Socialist Party)
UIL	Unione Italiana del Lavoro (Italian Union of Labour)

Map of Italy

1

The legacy of the past

Introduction

Italian unification in 1861 brought a series of geographical units under one rule. But it did not bring together their peoples. To paraphrase the famous words of the statesman D'Azeglio, it made Italy, but not Italians. Powerful internal divisions among the Italian population were not healed by unification. In many ways, in fact, they were intensified. These great internal conflicts and divisions were to have profound effects on the development and operation of the Italian political system.

Italy was divided first of all by social class. Peasants, landowners and gentry, industrialists, the liberal intelligentsia and industrial workers all had different interests, and sometimes these were sharply opposed. The peasantry demanded their own land to work, to sustain themselves and their families in dignity. Workers demanded higher wages, more holidays, better conditions of work. But these demands, of course, conflicted with the interests of the big landowners on the one hand and the industrialists on the other.

Another cleavage was caused by attitudes to religion and the clergy. Italy has only one major religion, Catholicism. But the profound opposition of the Church to secularisation, and the establishment of a State that challenged its authority over the people, produced a division between its most faithful adherents and anti-clericals, who saw the Church as an

1

essentially conservative and reactionary force. This division sometimes coincided with that of class, reinforcing it, but sometimes crossed class barriers, which helps to explain the success of the inter-class Catholic parties that have been so important in Italian politics.

Finally, Italy has remained characterised by a massive imbalance of wealth and resources between south and north. The Piedmontese leadership of unification, conscious of the landowning classes' key role in dealing with social unrest, upheld the traditional rights of propertied people and favoured the further concentration of land in their hands. By reinforcing the power of the landowners, unification helped to keep the south in a semi-feudal state, hindering the development of modern commerce and industry and dooming many of the southern people to a life of poverty and dependence on the central State.

Of course, some or all of these cleavages are present in other national societies. But in many countries, especially among Italy's northern neighbours, they were partly transcended by a sense of common nationhood, or mitigated by social reforms. In Italy, their starkness and persistence contributed to political instability and sharp repression. The way to the resolution of these conflicts was opened only after the defeat of Fascism and the restoration of democracy after the Second World War. And even then, their presence continued to be felt in strong class conflict, ideological division and polarisation, the prolonged resistance of profoundly conservative forces to the rapid modernisation of the country and the persistence of poverty in the south.

A new nation

Unlike other major European countries, such as France, Spain and the UK, Italy is relatively new as a nation State. As late as the mid-nineteenth century, until 1861, Italy was divided into a number of different units, ruled over by different powers:

- In the north-west was the Kingdom of Sardinia (Piedmont, Liguria, the Island of Sardinia and Nice and Savoy). Despite the name, Piedmont was the political centre of the Kingdom.
- The north-east (Lombardy and Venetia) was under Austrian occupation.
- The northern central part of the country was internally divided into duchies and principalities.
- In the centre, roughly coinciding with present-day Latium, were the Papal States.
- The south and Sicily – or the Kingdom of the Two Sicilies – was ruled by descendants of the Spanish Bourbon monarchy.

The national resurgence, or Risorgimento, was a movement to unite the different parts of Italy under one rule. It was led by the Piedmontese king Victor Emmanuel II and his Prime Minister Camillo Benso di Cavour, and supported latterly by the large landowners and middle classes. Earlier attempts at unification had ended in defeat. But critically, in 1859, Cavour and Victor Emmanuel were able to secure the support of France. In return for the territories of Nice and Savoy, France helped the Kingdom of Sardinia to force the Austrians to cede part of their territories, and in 1860 Napoleon III turned a blind eye when Piedmont annexed areas of the Papal States, where the French were garrisoned.

The intention of Cavour and Victor Emmanuel was to extend the Kingdom of Sardinia by annexation. But there was an alternative project of unification, one in which the peoples of Italy would found a new State and set up a new parliament and constituent assembly to establish its rules. The principal advocate of self-liberation and self-government by the peoples of Italy was the exile Giuseppe Mazzini, who believed that local insurrections could be used to force unification from the bottom up. Mazzini had a potential ally in the great soldier Giuseppe Garibaldi, and the course of Italian unification may well have been very different had the relationship between the two not been dogged by suspicion and misunderstanding.

In the spring of 1860, Garibaldi landed in Sicily with his famous thousand volunteers. Garibaldi was greeted as a liberator who would free the people from the rule of the Bourbons and return the land to those who worked it. Aided by popular insurrections, the Garibaldian forces soon controlled most of southern Italy. But despite his popularity and his success in bringing about the collapse of the Bourbon State in the south, Garibaldi was outmanoeuvred by the clever Cavour, who placed the Piedmontese army across his route to Rome and annexed most of the Papal States. Cavour organised plebiscites to join the southern territories, newly liberated by Garibaldi and his thousand, to Victor Emmanuel's regime, and Garibaldi had little option but to accept the Cavourian method of unification.

The Kingdom of Italy was proclaimed on 17 March 1861, although the future capital, Rome, was not reclaimed until 1870, when the French forces withdrew, as France was then under threat from Prussia.

The forcible annexation of Rome to the new Kingdom was taken by the Vatican as a profound insult. It symbolised a challenge to the authority of the Church which was to remain an open sore that delayed and complicated the development of popular political participation in Italy.

The difficulties of 'making Italians'

The unification of Italy was not so much the making of a nation as the imposition of a new set of rules and rulers from Piedmont. It was a revolution from outside. In the words of Antonio Gramsci, the great theorist and founding member of the Italian Communist Party, it was a 'passive revolution'. In this it was unlike the French Revolution, which had provided the French people with a message of political liberation and an enduring sense of their 'ownership' of the central State.

The widening north/south divide

The main axis on which unification was defended against the centrifugal tendencies within the new nation was a political alliance between northern industrialists and southern land-owners. It is in this alliance that many authors identify the origins of the continued economic disparity between north and south, a disparity that was aggravated over time by a continual haemorrhage of the south's most able and enter-prising people, forced off poor lands to seek opportunity abroad or in the north. The alliance was of central importance in perpetuating the political influence of a semi-feudal class of parasitic, largely absentee landlords, more interested in a life of ostentatious leisure than in the commercial development of the natural resources of the south. The so-called agrarian bloc, a parliamentary coalition of land-owning interests, was able to maintain a long-lasting veto on the land reforms that could have permitted the development of efficient commercial farms and the investment of the profits in new enterprises, techniques and technologies.

Garibaldi's early promise of a redistribution of land to the southern peasantry was never realised. On the contrary, it was the owners of the great estates who were the main beneficiar-ies of the sale, at bargain prices, of land seized from the religious orders during the annexation of the Papal States.

The northern middle classes also benefited from the alli-ance. The southern landlords ensured a supply of food to the growing urban centres of the north and they also guaranteed social order in the turbulent south. Political authority in the south was effectively devolved to the landowners and their agents, who used their virtual free rein in the administration of law for the harsh suppression of popular dissent. It was soon clear where the Piedmontese occupiers stood, as they came to the landowners' aid in the brutal suppression of peasant uprisings in 1860–5 and firmly defended the ancient rights of the feudalistic land-owning class. For most of the Italian peasantry, who at that time formed the bulk of the population, unification and the foundation of the nation of Italy meant little more than an additional source of oppression and taxation.

The liberal regime

The so-called liberal regime spanned the era between unification and the Fascist rise to power. It was a period of constitutional monarchy, through most of which parliament was elected from an extremely narrow franchise. Political parties were weak, undisciplined and indistinct, as ordinary people had little engagement with politics. Recruitment to political office was restricted to the elite, who had been the engine of unification.

The actual muscle of the unification movement was mainly supplied by young professional men and intellectuals, with some limited support from artisans. The industrial working class was, of course, still nascent and numerically limited. Even the emergent commercial and industrial middle classes of the north were not, at first, fully behind the movement for unification, although the Lombard industrialists later gave their support following a newspaper and leaflet campaign waged by landed proprietors and intellectuals. Italy, in fact, did not have a substantial and cohesive bourgeois class capable of generating a distinctively middle-class party that could have given effective leadership to the new regime.

From the turn of the century until 1914, Italian politics was dominated by the great statesman Giovanni Giolitti. Giolitti understood that the peasants and workers who formed the bulk of the population could not be dealt with by simple repression. For a while it appeared that Italy had a politician who could embody the national interest while quietly advancing the interests of a modern bourgeoisie. But these hopes foundered as Italy was dragged into the First World War and embarked on the road that would ultimately lead to Fascism.

The constitution

Italy's rulers after unification were not, of course, oblivious to the dangers faced by a regime whose legitimacy was so weakly established among its citizens. But the new regime proved unable to root the sense of national identity that could have permitted a self-confident State to nurture the development of an inclusive and accountable modern democracy. One gesture that might have gone some way towards creating a sense of belonging among the new citizens would have been to develop a new set of rules to govern and regulate the relationships between the various branches of government and the people they governed. But no new constitution followed the proclamation of the Kingdom of Italy. The old constitution of the Kingdom of Sardinia, granted in 1848 by King Charles Albert, remained current. The Statuto Albertino provided for a constitutional monarchy in which the King retained supreme executive power (in 1922, in fact, the monarch, faced with a situation of crisis, used these powers in a way that favoured Mussolini and the constitutional rise to power of Fascism). In a final insult, the King of the new State was still to be referred to as Victor Emmanuel II, a continuing reminder that no fresh pact with the people was to be forged.

The inability of the new Italian elite to develop a widespread sense of citizenship and belonging within the population had important consequences for the formative stages of the Italian political system and for the emerging relationships between the new State and its citizens. The fear that a devolution of power would help opponents of the regime to organise and undermine the legitimacy of the central State increased the determination of those who wanted to impose the highly centralised Piedmontese administrative system after 1861. Very little autonomy was granted to localities and it was in fact only in much more recent times – since the 1970s – that a process of devolution of power to the regional and local levels was put into effect.

Suffrage

A fear of the masses, verging on contempt, led to a very narrowly based franchise throughout most of the liberal era, at least until the electoral reform of 1912 under Prime Minister Giolitti. The prolonged exclusion of the great bulk of the population from the political process, followed by a sudden capitulation to pressure and a rapid, large-scale extension of the right to vote, placed the fragile regime under an enormous and ultimately unbearable strain.

In the early stages of the liberal regime, only educated males aged over twenty-five who were paying a property tax of 40 lire per year enjoyed the right to vote. In the elections of 1861, only 1.9 per cent of the population had the right to vote and only 57 per cent of the electorate actually exercised this right.

In 1882 an electoral reform extended the franchise to two million men, mostly from the urban middle class. Although suffrage was still very limited, it was now somewhat more difficult for the parliamentary notables and their supporters to rig the elections, and some radical and republican representatives were elected to the Chamber of Deputies alongside the Liberals.

In 1912, following an unpopular war of conquest in Libya, the franchise was extended to all men over thirty years of age and younger men who had served in the armed forces. This reform extended the right to vote to over 20 per cent of the Italian population and signalled the beginning of mass politics. Universal manhood suffrage was not introduced until 1919, under the fierce pressure of the men who had risked their lives for the nation in the First World War and who now demanded a say in its destiny. Women would have to await the end of the Second World War for their right to vote.

Politics

At least until the election of a number of Socialist deputies in the 1913 elections, parliament in the early liberal period was a rather exclusive assembly drawn from upper-middle-class Italians who had come to prominence during the unification movement. Political parties remained essentially parliamentary clubs with no functions of recruitment or political education and little organisation outside parliament. The weak development of organisation and discipline in the political parties was reinforced by the emergence of the practice of *trasformismo*, whereby majorities for the passage or veto of legislation were built by winning over deputies of whatever tendency with the promise of reward. Ministers regularly bought off, or 'transformed', parliamentary opposition by sharing out favours such as ministerial office. Such a system could work only in the presence of a narrow franchise that would ensure the election of representatives prepared to collude in this sort of practice.

It has been suggested that the exclusive and elitist nature of Italian politics in this formative period of the political system had a corrupting effect on politics and political leadership. Given the grip of the intelligentsia on political decision-making, it is perhaps unsurprising that they came to believe that history could and should be made by active minorities and that the masses could be held in contempt with impunity. It is notable that Vilfredo Pareto and Gaetano Mosca, the founding fathers of the elitism school in political sociology, were Italian. The belief that a small elite has the right and capacity to interpret the national interest on behalf of the people may also go some way to explain the appeal of Fascism among the Italian middle classes.

Church and State in the new nation

As in the French Revolution, the clergy were deeply hostile to the new secular State, which appeared as a direct challenge to the authority of the Vatican and its caste of clerics. The Pope, indeed, refused to recognise the Kingdom of Italy and religious citizens and leaders were forbidden by the Vatican to take any part in political activity. The *non expedit* decree issued after the occupation of Rome forbade believers to participate in national elections. Devout Catholics therefore remained outside or on the margins of the political life of the new State for many years to come.

From the first decade of the twentieth century, the *non expidit* was somewhat relaxed and Catholics began to give electoral support to the Liberal Party. In 1919, the Holy See gave its tacit approval to the Italian Popular Party (Partito Popolare Italiano, PPI) led by Don Sturzo, which won 20.5 per cent of the vote in the elections of that year. The PPI was the predecessor of the Christian Democrats (Democrazia Cristiana, DC), who were to dominate Italian political life after the Second World War. However, the Church's change of heart did not represent a genuine acceptance of the modern democratic State, but was rather a response to the growing appeal of socialism and fears that a continued detachment from the political life of the country would lead to the marginalisation of the Church.

The Church's antipathy to the secular liberal State was to be very damaging to the still fragile fabric of Italian democracy and contributed to its rupture by Fascism. Don Sturzo was committed to parliamentary democracy. However, his hopes for an alliance with anti-Fascist forces, including the Socialists, were effectively undermined by the opposition of the Pope. The Pope, in fact, welcomed the rise of Fascism, insofar as it meant the destruction of the hated liberal regime, and gave his support to the sections of the PPI that were less hostile to the Fascists. The full integration of the Catholic faithful into Italian political life was not formalised until the Concordat of 1929, a pact between the Fascist State and the Church, which effectively reversed Italy's status as a secular State.

The exclusion of religious citizens and leaders from political participation in the formative years of the new Kingdom was an important factor in the emergence of anti-clericalism as a force in modern Italian politics.

Foreign adventures

From the turn of the century, the liberal regime embarked on a course of imperial expansion and foreign war, at least in part as an attempt to unite the people in a patriotic ferment against a common external enemy. Italy, however, was not well placed to compete in the European scramble for colonial expansion. It did not enjoy the advantages of abundant natural resources and there was little development of the heavy industries needed to manufacture the armaments and means of transport required for warfare. The result of belligerent attitudes in a nation so poorly equipped to fight wars and win them was a series of ultimately humiliating adventures: the penetration of East Africa, ending with the Italian defeat at Aduwa; the successful but expensive invasion of Libya of 1911–12, and Italy's intervention in the First World War, with its outcome of 'mutilated victory' (Italy's failure to obtain further colonies or even to retain existing ones in Africa and the Middle East).

The Libyan war was launched in an attempt to appease right-wing and nationalist elements, but resulted in the profound alienation of the Socialists, whose moderate wing Giolitti had been attempting to woo with a programme of reform. The war was followed by an era of radicalisation in which the moderate leadership of the Socialists was largely defeated, or at least marginalised, by the radical 'maximalist' wing. The radicalisation of the Socialist Party disqualified it as a candidate for inclusion in the process of government and Giolitti abandoned his interest in it, turning his attention instead to the nationalist and Catholic vote.

The First World War and the polarisation of Italy

Italy's entrance into the First World War on the side of the allies was secretly negotiated by the executive, with the backing of the King, but against the wishes of the neutralist majority in parliament, including Giolitti. The polarisation of parliament reflected a broader division in the country at large, as a bitter debate raged over whether Italy should intervene in the war or remain neutral. The neutralists included most socialists, Catholics and liberals. The interventionists were a miscellaneous bunch including such powerful figures as Prime Minister Salandra and King Victor Emmanuel III. They were mainly conservatives and nationalists who hoped to acquire new territories for Italy as war spoil. However, a left-wing element among interventionists was made up of dissident, mainly southern, revolutionary socialists and syndicalists, who hoped that war would unleash revolution.

In April 1915 Italy committed itself to war. Nearly six million Italian men were conscripted into the army. They were mostly peasants; industrial workers were largely exempted because their work in the munitions factories was vital to the war effort. Half a million Italian soldiers died and many more were captured or wounded. The disproportionate burden of the costs of war born by the peasantry were to linger as a source of resentment long after the war had ended.

The resentment of the rural land workers was provoked further by the often contemptuous attitudes of the northern industrial working classes towards the demobilised soldiers. The working class had in large part remained in Italy during the war, carrying out essential war production, albeit under conditions of military discipline. The refusal of the largely neutralist working class to recognise the sacrifice made in the name of Italy by the peasant soldiery contributed to the left's difficulties in forging an alliance between workers and peasants during the revolutionary ferment of the immediate post-war period.

The liberal regime, following the First World War, was in deep difficulty. It had failed to widen the bases of its support by including a moderate Socialist Party in the process of government, because the reformists in the party leadership had lost the support of the rank and file. And attempts to unite the country in battles against external enemies and to whip up patriotic sentiments had succeeded only in deepening divisions within the new nation.

Mass parties and public participation in politics

So long as the great mass of the population remained rural and largely illiterate, it had been possible to exclude the representatives of the peasantry and emerging working classes from power. But as industrialisation and education spread and the pressures of modernisation grew stronger, it became increasingly difficult to resist growing demands for mass participation in politics.

The first stage in the transition to mass political participation was marked by the foundation of a party that could lay claim to the representation of the peasants and workers who made up the overwhelming bulk of the population. The Italian Socialist Party (Partito Socialista Italiano, PSI) was established in the 1880s and grew rapidly with the successive enlargements of the franchise.

In the absence of a well developed industrial, urbanised working class, the PSI had its social base in a sort of uneasy coalition of landless labourers, artisans, industrial workers and the educated middle class from which its leadership was drawn. The reformist leadership, however, proved unable to establish a disciplined and well financed party on the model of the German Social Democratic Party.

The rapid growth of the PSI and the emergence shortly after the turn of the century of an organised revolutionary faction within it were profoundly worrying to the Italian clergy. However, the emergence of a mass Catholic political party was initially hampered, as we have seen, by the *non expidit* forbidding Catholic participation in politics. But as the PSI grew, the Church's fear of subversion gained the upper hand over its antipathy towards the secular State and, with the tacit support of the Vatican, Don Sturzo's PPI gained a large following among the faithful, challenging the PSI for the hearts and minds of the people.

The aftermath of the war: the clash of left and right

Italy's short history was already a history of tension and conflict, in which the oppression of landlord and State was met with sporadic rebellions among the peasantry. But the peasant uprisings were largely spontaneous: they produced no disciplined organisation or coherent ideology with which to further the peasants' central cause – the redistribution of land. By the end of the First World War, however, Italy was equipped with a modern industrial working class, albeit a small one that was mostly concentrated in the so-called industrial triangle around Milan, Turin and Genoa, and a modern mass socialist party that could give leadership to the peasants' and workers' movements.

By comparison with the UK, Germany and even France, Italy was a late industrialiser. But the process of industrialisation was given a tremendous boost by Italy's entrance into the First World War, as industrial production was stepped up to provide the necessary materials of war, and the concentration of heavy, war-related industry increased. At the turn of the century, agriculture accounted for 51 per cent of Italian gross domestic product, while industry contributed a mere 20 per cent. By 1921, the contribution of agriculture had dropped to 34 per cent and the industrial and service sectors had grown concomitantly. In the north-western industrial triangle, the rapid development of modern iron and steel, engineering, shipbuilding, car-making, electricity and chemicals industries had led to the emergence of a relatively small but increasingly well organised working class.

Across Europe, the aftermath of the war was a period of economic and social turmoil. The revolution in Russia seemed to demonstrate that power really could be wrested from the hands of an exploitative ruling class and vested within the working class itself. For many Marxists and Socialists, the conditions for revolutionary upheaval seemed to be present in Italy, too. As in the rest of Europe, the economy had been heavily distorted by the needs of war production. It would take some time before industries, geared up to produce the means of war, could be converted to the normal production of goods for consumption. The consequent problems of shortages, inflation and unemployment were compounded by the return of soldiers from the front. The working classes were suffering very genuine economic hardship and their resentment was increased by the massive profits that had been made by industrialists during the war.

The combination of the hardship of the times and the hope in the future that seemed to be represented by the Bolshevik revolution was a powerful one, drawing thousands of new recruits to the main organisations of the working class. Between 1918 and 1920, membership of the trade unions had risen sharply: membership of the General Confederation of Workers (Confederazione Generale del Lavoro) had increased from 250,000 to over 2,000,000, while membership of the recently founded Catholic union had grown from 160,000 to over 1,000,000. Although the trade union leadership was not swept up in the revolutionary fervour of the times, it was increasingly unable to control the enthusiasm of its base. Strikes, demonstrations, food riots and occupations broke out with increasing intensity all over Italy, particularly in the industrial triangle and the more advanced agricultural areas of Emilia-Romagna and Tuscany. The unrest culminated in the so-called *Biennio Rosso* – two red years – in which factories were occupied and turned over to worker management while, in a separate movement, land belonging to the great estates was taken over by the peasants.

As the waves of increasingly violent left-wing protest grew to their crescendo, conservative fears of an imminent Bolshevik revolution in Italy deepened.

The conservative backlash and the rise of Fascism

In March 1919, the ex-Socialist Benito Mussolini founded the Fascio di Combattimento (Combat Group) from a mixed social base. The membership included war veterans, especially ex-officers embittered by Italy's 'mutilated victory' in the war, urban professionals and white-collar workers, landowners, wealthy peasants and estate managers. The Fascist squads were welcomed by the rural landlords, especially in the country-side of Emilia-Romagna and Tuscany, as the means to break new contracts which had been forced on them by the increasing militancy of the rural workers. Over the period 1919–20, land workers had won an eight-hour working day, substantial wage increases for day labourers and the right to organise in trade unions. Peasant tenants had also gained guarantees of tenure, a significant voice in estate management and the elimination of remaining feudal obligations. To the horror of the landowners, the PSI was even calling for a legal obligation on them to employ a certain number of workers per hectare of land owned. The world of the landed gentry was being turned upside down; together the new contracts and demands would constitute a very significant limit on the owners' traditional ability to dispose of land and labour as they saw fit.

The main targets of the Fascist squads were the PSI and the trade unions. The authorities and police turned a blind eye on the activities of the squads; indeed, off-duty policemen often participated in them. By 1922, Fascist organisations were firmly established in most areas of the north and centre.

The Fascist movement was generously financed by rich agrarians and industrialists, who in some cases even provided Fascist bands with horses, rifles and motor cars and gave them the names of 'targets'. Profits were being seriously threatened by the powerful urban and rural workers' movements, and landowners and entrepreneurs were increasingly frustrated by the government's failure to intervene decisively to put a halt to the waves of strikes and occupations. Thus Italy's bourgeoisie collaborated in the rise of Fascism. Initially, however, they foresaw no more than a temporary Fascist participation in government.

Mussolini's accession to power

Had it not been for the complacency and disunity of the potential opposition to Fascism, Mussolini and the Fascists may never have acquired full control over the State. Mussolini rose to power by means that were never wholly unconstitutional. The famous March on Rome of October 1922 was not in fact a coup d'état. About 30,000 activists took part in it and, given sufficient political will, it undoubtedly could have been dispersed. In fact, the Prime Minister, Luigi Facta, requested the King to order troops to turn the march away, but the King ultimately decided against this, perhaps fearing mutiny or the outbreak of civil war.

Mussolini had made it known that he would not participate in a government of which he was not Prime Minister and was in fact offered the post late in October, even before the March on Rome. He presided over a coalition government – including the PPI – until the so-called Aventine secession in August 1924, when the 'democratic forces' (deputies) withdrew from parliament following the discovery of the body of a moderate Socialist who had been murdered by Fascist thugs. Mussolini panicked and would have resigned had the King required it. However, the conservative forces inside and outside parliament did not abandon Mussolini, and the Aventine secession marked the beginning of the end for legal opposition to Fascism.

For a long period of time, then, Mussolini was able to use his leadership of a constitutionally legal government to entrench his power. How was this possible? The answer to this question lies less in Mussolini's strength than in the weakness and division of the parties opposed to him. In 1923, the PPI was ejected from the governing coalition and began to fall apart as a political force. The PPI, founded as the party of Catholics, had lost the support of the Vatican, which was now pro-Fascist, convinced not by ideology but by the promise of a new and more powerful role in society. The left was weakened by the prolonged Fascist onslaught on its organisations and was deeply divided by the schism of part of the PSI, which led to the formation of the Communist Party in January 1921. To simplify a complex question, Mussolini was able to come to power because the non-Fascist forces of the establishment believed that he could be 'used' to defeat the left once and for all, and then contained. But they bided their time too long, until Mussolini and the Fascists were no longer containable.

The nature of Fascism

Under the Fascist regime, all political opposition, as well as independent trade unions, were banned and political partici- pation was restricted to the National Fascist Party and its organisations, such as the Fascist trade union organisation and youth movements. Elected local governments were re- placed by appointed officials. The Fascists also took control over the press, establishing stringent censorship. A secret po- lice organisation (the Organisation for Surveillance and the Repression of Anti-Fascism) was established and the govern- ment's powers of arrest and detention were extended. The death penalty became available for a wider range of crimes and a special court was set up to deal with political crimes.

However, Italian Fascism was not fully totalitarian. Fascism lacked the consensus that could have allowed a total de- naturing of the social fabric and the imposition of a single source of authority. Several forces in Italian society retained a relative independence of action vis-à-vis the Fascist State. Notable among these was the Catholic Church. Fascism was forced into an accommodation with the Church. Catholicism was, of course, deeply entrenched in Italy and there was virtually no area of public or private life in which its organ- isations were not active. Even had he wanted to, Mussolini could not have mounted an effective challenge to the national and international power represented by the Pope in Rome. Instead, he negotiated a compromise settlement, in the form of the Concordat of 1929, which gave Church and State 'in- dependent and sovereign' status within their own ambits. Catholicism thus remained the official State religion. The agreement permitted the Church to retain its very wide role in the life of Italian society, especially in education and, through its charitable activities, in social welfare. The Concordat also made a substantial financial settlement on the Church, laying the basis for its global financial role.

Employers were also able to hold on to a considerable degree of autonomy from State regulation, especially through the twenty-two 'mixed corporations' of employers and employees set up in 1934 and empowered to determine wages and conditions within specific sectors. From 1928, workers' elements within employer/employee structures had been staffed not by real workers' representatives but by Fascist officials, who were usually sympathetic to the employers' interests. Furthermore, Confindustria, the main employers' association, could deal directly with government.

The fall of Fascism

Mussolini's decision to enter the Second World War was ultimately fatal for Italian Fascism. The Italian forces were humiliated in Greece and Africa and support for the regime crumbled under the combined pressures of bombardment, food shortages and rising prices. From spring 1943, opposition to Fascism appeared in the open strikes, protest and industrial sabotage movements in the northern industrialised areas. These movements had an important effect in weakening the economic and social structures of Fascism and preparing the way for the Allied advance.

On 10 July 1943, the Allies landed in Sicily. On 25 July, the Fascist Grand Council deposed Mussolini and the King requested his resignation. Mussolini was arrested and a new government was established under Marshal Badoglio. The end of Fascism was celebrated with mass demonstrations. Everywhere, Fascist insignia were removed from buildings and monuments, and Fascist Party headquarters were burned.

But Italy had not yet changed sides in the war. For a while, the monarchy and army procrastinated, negotiating with the Allies while promising Germany continued support. In the meantime, in August, German troops moved into Italy. At last, on 3 September 1943, a secret armistice was signed between Italy and the Allies, and was made public on 8 September. King Victor Emmanuel and Marshal Badoglio flew to Brindisi and the army was dissolved. Mussolini was rescued by a German parachute action and was taken north to head the puppet Republic of Salò. Italy was now divided in two, with the allies advancing from the south and the industrial north occupied by the Germans.

Political life resumed in the traditionally more conservative south on the basis of the nuclei of the leading parties which had survived Fascism. The resumption of political life in the north, where strong residues of Communist and Socialist organisation had been strengthened by the prestige of the left-dominated partisan movements, had to await full liberation – by which time the new political structures were already firmly established in the south.

The legacies of Fascism

One of the main legacies of Italian Fascism for post-war democracy in Italy was the enhanced power of the Church in educational and family matters; in the wealth of Catholic organisations that could be used for ideological purposes; and in the concomitant weakening of the institutions of the labour movement. Through its annihilation of non-Fascist institutions, especially those associated with political parties and trade unions, Fascism created a sort of associational vacuum. The one exception to this was, of course, the associations of the Catholic Church, which remained intact as a dense network of support for the DC after the Second World War. Especially important was Catholic Action, whose continued activities through the 1930s provided a training ground for many of the DC's future leading politicians.

Another Fascist legacy that helped shape the future of Italian post-war politics was the nucleus of the public sector.

In the 1920s the State took into ownership a number of banks and their manufacturing subsidiaries. In 1933, in the midst of the depression, the Institute for Industrial Reconstruction (Istituto per la Ricostruzione Industriale, IRI) was set up to ward off mass redundancies following a wave of bankruptcies. The IRI was a State-owned holding company, which bought up shares in failing enterprises. By 1940, about one-fifth of all capital assets in joint-stock corporations in Italy were controlled by the IRI, and important sectors such as iron, steel, shipbuilding and banking were in this way effectively monopolised by the State.

After the end of Fascism and the war, the IRI became the model for a novel approach to economic management in which the State avoided direct nationalisation by using its influence over the companies in which the IRI owned shares to shape and direct post-war economic growth. The resources of the giant public sector that was thus created later became a major source of patronage and clientelism, in which party notables exchanged jobs and favours for political support.

Fascism also gave initial form to the Italian welfare state. In response to the 1930s depression, many of the mainly voluntary social insurance schemes of the liberal era were made statutory and broadened to include more of the population. Large sectoral agencies, administratively independent of the State, were created to collect compulsory contributions and manage the provision of services and pensions. These agencies remained, together with the Catholic associations, as the basis of the post-war Italian welfare system.

Fascism also left a legacy in the centralised administrative system, which would for long remain under the influence of Fascist residues within it; in the strong conservative and reactionary strands that remained embedded in the military and secret services; and in a potentially repressive legal code that to this day has not been cleared from the statute books.

All these influences have combined with still earlier legacies, such as Italy's sharp ideological divisions, to place an enormous burden on the democratic Republic that emerged from the Second World War, helping to warp the liberal and democratic intentions of the Constituent Assembly which framed the 1948 constitution of the new Republic.

Further reading

Blinkhorn, M. *Mussolini and Fascist Italy*, London (1994).
Clark, M. *Modern Italy 1871–1982*, London (1984).
Mack Smith, D. *Italy: A Modern History*, Michigan (1969).
Woolf, S. J. (ed.) *The Rebirth of Italy 1943–1950*, London (1972).
Zariski, R. *Italy: The Politics of Uneven Development*, Hinsdale, Illinois (1972).

2

The constitution and institutional arrangements

Introduction

Italy's first constitution was effectively imposed on the people after unification by the Piedmontese rulers of the Kingdom of Sardinia. In contrast, its second, anti-Fascist and republican constitution was drawn up in the Constituent Assembly by elected representatives and signalled a net rejection of authoritarian rule. Now, following the devastating Italian corruption scandals of the early 1990s, which brought domestic instability and international disgrace, Italy is once more in search of a fresh start.

The major ills of the post-war Italian political system – immobilism and cabinet instability, 'rule by the parties' and the domination of politics by a small and increasingly corrupt caste of politicians – are variously attributed to liberal constitutional principles that guard against an over-centralisation of power in the executive. Pressure has grown for an accountable executive powerful enough to short-cut the lengthy, complex and highly negotiated decision-making procedures. But the Italian constitution has been gradually moulded into its present interpretation by a variety of social forces over almost fifty years. A quick institutional fix may not have the intended consequences. There are many facets of Italy's present constitution that may be sorely missed in the event of a rush to simplistic and illiberal solutions.

The Constituent Assembly, 1946–8

On 2 June 1946, the Italian people, for the first time ever including women, were asked to participate in the first free general elections for over twenty years. Their opinion was being polled on two issues that would be crucial in shaping the democracy that was to be built on the ashes of Fascism. The first poll was a referendum to decide whether Italy should retain the monarchy, disgraced by its collusion in Fascism, or set up a republic. The second was to elect the Constituent Assembly, whose task was to draw up a new constitution for Italy to replace the Statuto Albertino, which had been imposed on the new united Italy by its Piedmont-based ruling class in 1861. In the referendum, the country voted for the republican form. The vote was fairly close run, as support for the monarchy remained high in the south, where the peasantry had been very dependent on its largesse.

Elections to the Constituent Assembly resulted in a coalition of anti-Fascist forces. The DC (the successor to the PPI), with 35.2 per cent of the vote and 207 seats, emerged as the largest party in the Assembly, but electoral support for the PSI (20.7 per cent) and the Communist Party (Partito Comunista Italiano, PCI) (19 per cent) was strong, ensuring considerable left influence in the framing of the rules that would govern relations between State and citizens in the new Republic.

The constitution was drawn up by a commission of seventy-five, divided into three subcommittees. The party composition of the committees reflected the proportion of votes received by each. For the next eighteen months, the elected representatives of the Italian people set about the task of drawing up a constitution that could enshrine in law the human and civil rights of the Republic's citizens, ensure that the voices of all, including minorities, would be heard, and safeguard the people against the rise of another dictatorship.

The philosophy of the constitution

The formal document that finally emerged from the debates of the founding fathers (as opposed to the *real* organisation of powers that developed in the 'blocked' democracy) has been defined as one of the key documents shaping the democratic identity of the post-war West through the negation of Nazism and Fascism. The intention of the Constituent Assembly was to spread State powers as widely as possible, to ensure the broadest possible access to public decision-making and to guard against the concentration of powers in the hands of the few. The executive was therefore subject to an array of checks and balances, its powers diluted by the need to negotiate its legislative programmes through a powerful, bicameral parliament and gain the approval of a constitutional court. The anti-Fascist philosophy of an inclusive governing process with a wide dispersal of powers went through despite heavy pressure on the DC from the Church to opt for a presidential form of government with a powerful executive.

The constitution and the 'Catho–Communist' divide

Italian social history has been marked by the stand-off between two major forces whose mutual hostility still today scars the Italian body politic. Particularly in the north and centre of Italy, political life has been shaped and grounded within two major camps, the 'red' Marxist and anti-clerical subculture, strongest in the centre and industrial north-west, and the 'white' Catholic and anti-Communist subculture, with its heartlands in the north-east. Although these opposed subcultures have both shrunk and relaxed over the course of time, the clash between them has been central to the evolution of post-war society in Italy.

The constitution seemed – at first – to hold out the promise that the two sides could be reconciled and that one would not have to suffer defeat and exclusion at the hands of the other.

For the first time, Italy had a constitution that was forged through a process of negotiation among a group of people who were broadly representative of the different interests present in the nation as a whole. The result was a document based on compromise, which protected and enshrined the rights of workers and of the Catholic Church and its faithful.

A Republic founded on labour

The imprint of the left on the constitution is seen especially in the prominence afforded to the citizen as employee and the special protections given to workers. The constitution states in its opening passages that 'Italy is a democratic Republic founded on labour'. It goes on to affirm the right to work, to guarantee trade union rights and to enshrine employee rights to a voice in the management of the workplace.

The progressive substance of the institutional arrangements set out in the constitution and the ideals embodied especially in its first part help explain why the PCI, unlike some other West European Communist parties of the time, adopted a gradualist strategy towards the achievement of socialism, in which the framework of liberal democracy would be accepted. The PCI took considerable pride in the constitution it had helped to frame. The leadership retained a profound faith in the possibility of socialist development within the constitutional framework, even through the long period of DC domination of the political system.

The constitution, and the part played in its drafting by the left, strengthened the Communist leadership's claim that they were not a danger to democracy and would abide by the democratic judgement of the people should they ever be elected to government. However, this claim was not everywhere believed.

State and Church in the constitution

The constitution also contained generous concessions to the Catholic Church. It will be remembered that the Vatican had denied participation in the political life of the nation to the faithful with the *non expedit*. Although the admonition had been relaxed in the first decades of the twentieth century to allow the formation of Don Sturzo's PPI, the Church gave its formal recognition of the secular state only under Fascism. The Church's full adherence to and participation in the democracy established with the constitution of 1948 was secured by the inclusion within it of the Concordat signed between Church and Mussolini in 1929. This gave the Church very important powers in Italian affairs. It ensured continued Church control over marriages and gave it special financial concessions and a monopoly over religious education in State schools. The Concordat was included without amendment and with the support even of the supposedly anti-clerical PCI, in what was perhaps a gesture of goodwill by a leadership hoping for an extension of the experiment with tripartite government including the PCI and the PSI. If this is so, it was a forlorn hope.

In May 1947, the left was ejected from the cabinet. In the general election of April 1948 the DC gained an absolute majority in the Chamber of Deputies, but decided to govern with the help of the lay parties. The pattern of coalitions excluding the major party of the left was now established. With the partial exception of the governments of national unity of 1976–9, the left would have to wait until the historic election of April 1996 before it could take its turn in government.

The completion of the constitution

On paper, the 1948 constitution is an impressive testimony to the liberal, anti-Fascist and even progressive values on which the emergent democracy was founded. However, hopes in the progressive elements of the constitution were dealt a mortal blow by a Supreme Court decision in February 1948 to make a distinction between parts of the constitution for immediate implementation and a 'programmatic' part, to be realised at some time in the future.

Following the ousting of the PCI from the tripartite government in 1947, the DC began its long-lasting domination of Italian politics. From its position of power, the party, and especially its right wing, was able to resist and delay the establishment of important institutions and rights that could have been used to mount effective challenges to its authority. The Constitutional Court was not established until 1956 and regional autonomy and the right to hold referendums were put on hold until 1970. The Workers' Statute, passed in 1970, can also be seen as a final enactment of constitutional principles concerning the protection of trade union rights. The eventual enablement of parts of the constitution that had been for so long suspended was in large part the product of the growing power and anger, especially from the 1960s, of social movements representing sectors of the population who were not the natural constituencies of the DC and who suffered most from the DC's prolonged domination of the political system.

The institutions of the 1948 constitution

The electoral system

Italy's electoral system is not technically established in the constitution, but will be treated here for convenience.

Before important reforms in 1993, Italy's system of proportional representation (PR) was very pure. Even parties gaining a share of the vote as low as 2 per cent could take up that proportion of the seats in parliament. These rules facilitate (although they do not create) a multi-party system, by giving an incentive to vote even for small parties. In a PR system every vote counts and electors have a real chance of electing members of parliament (MPs) of the party that most closely represents their views, even if that party is small.

A multi-party system with PR is often associated with coalition governments, as no single party gains enough parliamentary seats to govern alone. Under certain circumstances this can give considerable or even undue power to a party that obtained a relatively small percentage of the national vote. It may, for example, be necessary to include the small party in the coalition to ensure a governing majority in parliament. In this way, the smaller 'lay' parties of liberal tradition, and later the PSI, were regularly included in Italian governing coalitions. In Germany, too, the small Liberal Party is a normal component of governing coalitions of the right and left. Even when a small party is not actually included in the coalition, the government may still need its votes to ensure the passage of legislation. The small party's support may then be offered in return for concessions. Systems in which a very large number of parties compete can also give rise to instability, as withdrawal of support by one party can lead to the collapse of the government. Although this has been a problem in Italy, it is not necessarily the case, as a number of multi-party systems with relative cabinet stability attest.

Systems of PR contrast with plurality or 'first-past-the-post' systems such as that in the UK. This sort of electoral mechanism is often associated with party systems in which there are only two potential parties of government, as only one candidate in a constituency, the one with the most votes, can win. Small parties cannot win seats unless their support is concentrated in a particular geographical area, as in the case of the UK nationalist parties. Because of this, many potential supporters of small parties give their vote to the 'least bad' of the two main parties. A pure two-party system would give rise to government by a single party that would have no need to negotiate or compromise with its defeated rival.

The President of the Republic

The President is indirectly elected by both houses of parliament (see below) and three delegates from each region. Thus the President does not have a direct popular mandate and the authority of the post is consequently limited. Under normal circumstances, the President's main job is to carry out the ceremonial tasks of the head of State. However, the President is not entirely a figurehead and is more powerful than a constitutional monarch such as the British.

The powers of the President include:

- The designation of the Prime Minister. The President must, of course, choose someone who will be able to form a government, in other words a leading politician from a major party who is capable of putting together a coalition that will have the support of the majority of MPs. Normally, therefore, the President does not have a real choice. But despite this very important limitation, the power to designate the Prime Minister can give the President some influence in the complex negotiations that precede the formation of a government.
- The power to dissolve parliament and call elections when a government loses its working majority and cannot continue in power. However, the President must consult with both houses before dissolving the legislature. Once again, the decision to dissolve parliament is not really made by the President.
- A suspensive veto. This means that the President can send a law back to parliament unsigned, accompanied by an explanation of why approval is being denied. This veto can be overridden by parliament with a simple majority vote, but can mean a bill's death.
- The nomination of five (of fifteen) judges to the Constitutional Court and five life senators.

The real influence of the President depends a great deal on both personality and circumstance. The office of Presidency has a high profile and is generally revered. The President's public speeches and addresses receive a great deal of attention in the media and have weight with public opinion.

Although the President is chosen by the usual process of negotiation among party influentials, he or she is expected, once elected, to be *super partes*, or above party politics. However, Presidents have sometimes used their influence to give voice to their own political opinions. In the 1980s, for example, President Francesco Cossiga became famous for his controversial outbursts.

Especially in times of difficulty, the President can wield a power that goes well beyond the ceremonial and purely figurehead role of head of State. As the President is theoretically above politics, he or she will not automatically be supportive of the executive and may even admonish the Prime Minister and colleagues in government and recall them to their constitutional duties. This potential of the office was demonstrated during the short-lived government of the media tycoon Silvio Berlusconi in 1994, which was marked by an increasingly bitter antagonism between the Prime Minister and President Oscar Luigi Scalfaro. In this period, the President emerged as a sort of guarantor and interpreter of the constitution.

The Prime Minister (President of the Council of Ministers)

The Italian Prime Minister, whose office is located in Palazzo Chigi in Rome, does not have to be the leader of the biggest party in parliament. In fact, in the convention of the DC, the Prime Minister was never the official party leader.

The Prime Minister is designated by the President, after the general election, following a complex process of negotiation. At least until the 1993 reforms of the electoral system, the electorate had no way of knowing, at the time of the ballot, who would be leading the next government. This reinforced the importance of the party over the individual, as the electorate had to vote for the party of their choice rather than its leading personalities.

Once the Prime Minister has been designated, she or he must consult the party and faction leaders to canvass their support for the government, and then form the Council of

Ministers, or cabinet. In reality, the Prime Minister's discretion in this exercise is very limited, as the overriding problem is how to secure and maintain a majority of parliamentary votes. Ministerial and other key positions are often allocated to appease potential dissidents by 'buying' their support. In fact, party or faction leaders often stipulate the appointment of individuals to particular cabinet positions as a precondition for supporting the government. As a result, the first allegiance of ministers is often to the party influentials who secured their jobs for them, not to the Prime Minister. Unlike a British counterpart, the Italian Prime Minister does not necessarily have a collegiate and supportive cabinet. Furthermore, the Prime Minister cannot sack a minister. Even if dismissal were possible, it would risk the parliamentary majority that was pieced together through the painstaking process of negotiation. There are, therefore, no effective sanctions against unruly and outspoken colleagues in cabinet.

The Italian Prime Minister is thus very weak in relation to parliament. The loss of the support of a single powerful faction leader may in some cases be sufficient for the government to lose its parliamentary majority, leaving the Prime Minister no option but to resign. This gives a considerable power to party and faction leaders inside and outside the governing coalition. It also means that a Prime Minister's tenure in office may be extremely brief: the average life of Italian governments during the first republic has been about ten months.

The power of influential party politicians, or notables, which is independent of the political executive, is a component of the concept of party rule or 'particracy' – the form of government that has been characteristic of much of the post-war period in Italy. The concept of 'particracy' is more fully explained on page 69.

If the government can no longer command a majority in parliament, the President has to designate another Prime Minister to piece together a viable coalition. In some cases, the same person is designated and the cabinet is simply reshuffled to accommodate the ambitions of the party bosses and the shifting balance of power among them. Once a government falls, it generally takes about six weeks to negotiate a new one.

The cabinet in Italy tends to be large, including at least twenty ministers with portfolio and a handful without. The oversized cabinets reflect the need to offer something to all the leading politicians whose support is essential for the survival of the coalition.

The legislature (houses of parliament)

Italy has a bicameral system, in other words the legislature is divided into two houses. The upper house (Senate) has 315 members and is located in Palazzo Madama; the lower house (Chamber of Deputies) has 630 members and is located in Palazzo Montecitorio.

The Italian legislature is an example of co-equal bicameralism, the two chambers having equal powers. This contrasts with the situation in the UK, where the upper house (House of Lords) is relatively feeble in relation to the lower house. In Italy, both chambers must pass a bill in an identical form before it becomes law. Unlike in the USA or Germany, there is no coordinating committee to reconcile legislation that has been even slightly amended in one of the houses. This means that both chambers have the power to veto legislation, making it difficult for the government to get its programme through in unamended form.

These difficulties were even more acute before the late 1980s, when voting on bills, and even on their component clauses, was frequently by secret ballot. This meant that neither party leaderships nor citizens could be sure how MPs had voted. It was therefore impossible to ensure a disciplined pro-government vote by all the parliamentarians of the governing coalition. This contrasts very strongly with a system such as that in the UK, where a government with a majority in the House of Commons can rely on disciplined voting, reinforced by the whips, and can therefore steer its programme through the legislature with little fear of unwanted amendment.

The existence of backbench rebels, or 'snipers', voting against government measures increased the difficulties experienced by Prime Ministers in trying to establish discipline within the governing coalition. As loyalty cannot be demonstrated, it cannot be rewarded by promotion. Politicians' careers depend less on reliable service to the elected government they are supposed to be supporting than on the personal support that they can muster, by whatever means, inside and outside parliament.

In 1988, the use of secret ballots in parliament was largely abolished. It is now used mostly for issues involving personal ethical and moral positions.

The committee system

Members of parliament are organised in permanent committees paralleling the government ministries. The president of each house (an office similar to the British Speaker) divides parliamentary work up among the committees. The committees are very powerful as, uniquely in Europe, they can pass a wide range of legislation directly into law, or veto it, without referring it back to the floor of house. In fact, only issues relating to the constitution, voting rights, international agreements and the budget must be dealt with by the full house.

As a result, the Italian parliament's output of legislation is greater than that of any other post-war European legislature and a large part of this output is in the form of so-called *leggine* (little laws), passed in the committees and mostly relating to special interests. This power of the standing committees makes them a focus of attention for private businesses, which can try to influence them to pass 'pork barrel' legislation that will favour their particular interests.

The committee system was also one of the ways in which the PCI was able to influence legislation despite its historic exclusion from government. The PCI could have blocked much of the committees' output of little laws, as their approval requires a majority of four-fifths and Communists made up nearly one-third of MPs and consequently of committee members. However, the PCI frequently refrained from using its veto power and, in turn, the legislation that it proposed was also not always rejected out of hand.

Relations between executive and legislature

The Italian legislature is extremely powerful in relation to the government. Without a large consensus, a rarity in Italy's fragmented politics, it is extremely difficult for the government to get its planned legislation through both houses of parliament intact. The government's position is further weakened because its bills have no special status over private members' bills. Government-sponsored bills may be amended or rejected by the legislature and there is no limit on the private members' bills that may be introduced by individual backbench MPs.

Finally, there is no protection for government when its majority is lost. This contrasts, for example, to the system in Germany, where the legislature must be able to agree on a new government before the current one can fall (the so-called constructive vote of confidence).

Government difficulties were exacerbated as the dominant position of the DC was progressively undermined from the late 1960s. Increasingly, governments were forced to exploit a procedure that is subversive of the executive-restraining intentions of the constitution. In Italy, as in France, parliament can be bypassed by the issue of decree laws. This constitutional loophole was intended to give the government special powers in times of emergency, but has been used with increasing frequency since the 1970s in a wide range of policy spheres. Decree laws have to be enacted by parliament into ordinary law within sixty days. In fact, parliament often refuses to convert decrees into law, sometimes bargaining with the government to get them modified. However, in a practice that has become increasingly common, decrees can simply be reissued if parliament refuses their ratification.

The judiciary

Another important check on executive power established by the constitution is the judiciary. According to the constitution the judiciary is independent of any other power. It is controlled by an independent body, the High Council of the Judiciary, which is made up of judges, lawyers and legal experts and is presided over by the President of the Republic. Ten members are chosen by parliament and twenty by the magistrates themselves. It is the High Council, not the government's Ministry of Justice, that oversees recruitment, promotion and discipline procedures in the judiciary.

Despite its theoretical insulation from politics, the judiciary is – or was – permeated by the same kinds of party and faction allegiances that run through all other Italian institutions. Promotions within the judiciary were frequently based not on seniority or merit, but on agreements among political factions in the High Council of the Judiciary and in the parties. This, indeed, is part of the reason why systemic corruption continued largely undisturbed by judicial investigation for so long. The networks linking factions in the judiciary and the parties could be used to call in favours and protect the corrupt.

The parties' hold on the judiciary weakened in the early 1990s. Following the fall of Communism in Eastern Europe, the rhetoric of anti-Communism was less compelling. The DC began to lose the automatic support it had enjoyed by virtue of being the main bulwark against Communism and attitudes to it became more openly critical. At the same time, electoral support for the Northern League – then emerging as an alternative party of the middle classes – was rising and corruption, especially within the sprawling, inefficient public sector from which the Rome-based parties fed, became one of its central issues. The rise of this new party helped to provide the political space for independent groupings of magistrates such as those of the so-called Mani Pulite (Clean Hands) team to engage in a sustained effort to expose the corrupt intertwining of business and the State.

Now that the influence of parties on the judiciary appears to have loosened and the magistrates are playing a more independent role, their powers have been coming in for a great deal of critical attention. The powers of Italian magistrates to hold and question suspects before trial have been the subject of particularly fierce debate. In the 1970s, these powers were most frequently used against the left and were an important weapon against the leaderships of the social movements that had seemed to threaten the Italian establishment at that time. But at the height of the corruption scandals of the early 1990s, the typical suspect in preventive custody was from a very different background. Top-level managers of the giant State enterprises, party notables and previously respected business people were now experiencing the hospitality of the police cell and the attentions of the investigating magistrates. For many, the indignity and shame proved too much and a rash of suicides among the illustrious detainees sparked calls for limitations on the magistrates' powers.

There can be little doubt that in some cases the new concern for the civil rights of those held in preventive detention masks a more self-interested desire to see the corruption investigations wound down and the whole issue of corruption allowed quietly to disappear. The magistrates themselves argue that their powers to detain persons who might otherwise tamper with evidence are vital for the continuation of the struggle against corruption. Certainly, the power to hold and question suspects helped the magistrates to obtain the voluminous confessions that implicated ever-widening circles of business and political elites and threatened the rule of the parties in the early 1990s. However, the civil rights aspect is an important one. The magistrates' draconian powers sit ill with a genuinely democratic republic that is respectful of human rights.

The Constitutional Court

The Constitutional Court, which was only established in 1956, has come to be seen as a chief defender of the values of the 1948 constitution. Its main task is to judge the constitutionality of existing law. Before the Court was set up, this responsibility fell to the notoriously conservative Court of Cassation, the highest court of appeal for matters of ordinary law. The Court of Cassation was often unwilling to find pre-Republican law unconstitutional and the result was a backlog of Fascist legislation that has not been removed to this day. Attacking this backlog took up most of the Court's time in its earlier years.

Like all Italian institutions, the Constitutional Court is not entirely free from political influence. Five each of its fifteen judges are chosen by the President of the Republic, parliament and the ordinary and administrative high courts. The parliamentary nominees, especially, tend to be party political. The range of parties included in the distribution of seats on the Constitutional Court widened over time with the widening of the range of parties included in the governing coalitions. From the 1960s, the PCI was also included in the distribution. Despite this politicisation and its very large workload, the Court has proved an effective check on the executive, overturning or forcing the reinterpretation of laws it judges incompatible with the constitution.

The Constitutional Court has acquired some new functions since 1956 and especially since the implementation in 1970 of the ordinary regions (see chapter 5) and of referendums. The Court must resolve conflicts of competence between different branches of the State and is frequently called on to adjudicate disputes between region and State as to which level of government is responsible for what. The Court must also rule on the admissibility of questions to be put to referendum.

Referendums

Provision for referendums was made in the 1948 constitution, but was not enabled until 1970. Referendums in Italy are normally abrogative. In other words, they can repeal laws or parts of laws, but they cannot propose new law. This negative power of referendums can make them a rather clumsy instrument. For example, the 1993 referendum intended to reduce the importance of PR in all parliamentary elections, but approved only changes to the Senate. This was because elections to the Chamber of Deputies have different rules that could not readily be adapted to reduce the importance of PR through a mechanism of repeal.

However, referendums are a powerful expression of public feeling and politicians must take note of the general intention behind them. The 1993 referendum on electoral reform, which was combined with other referendums expressing dissent towards the system, forced the resignation of the Prime Minister, Giuliano Amato. Amato had understood that the referendums were a death sentence for the regime. Before this, in 1991, the referendum on preference voting had signalled the beginning of a mass, cross-party movement for electoral and system reform.

Referendums have been promoted on a wide range of issues. Some of the most important of these include divorce, public order legislation, public financing of parties, abortion, wage indexation, nuclear power, field sports, electoral law and drug decriminalisation. Referendums tend to be associated with anti-establishment themes, in which the promoters' intent is to liberalise law or defend permissive legislation. As such, they were a major tool of the Radical Party, with its concern for civil rights, and later the Greens. More recently, as noted above, referendums have been used to express public outrage at the corruption and inefficiency of the regime. However, referendums are not always anti-establishment. The 1974 divorce referendum – the first to be held since the establishment of the 1948 constitution – was promoted by militant Catholics who wanted the repeal of a law permitting divorce.

Referendums can be called at the request of 500,000 voters or five regional councils and must then be allowed by the Constitutional Court.

Electoral and institutional change: the 'Second Republic'

Italy is currently undergoing a major process of institutional reform. New electoral rules have already been established, although further amendment of these is possible. However, the impact of the 1993 electoral reforms on the underlying philosophy of the constitution was so great that many already speak of a 'Second Republic'. Actual constitutional reform, which is more difficult to achieve, is in progress.

Although the reform of Italy's constitutional arrangements and electoral system has long been debated, it was not until the corruption scandals of 1992–3 and the mass shunning of the traditional parties by the electorate that much was actually done. Until the crisis of the 1990s, those who had the power to change the rules were on the whole served well enough by the existing ones.

Electoral reform

This section will be limited to a description of the rule changes brought in in 1993. The social and political movement that led to the reform is described in chapter 4, on the old regime, while the effects so far of the changes on the political system are analysed in chapter 8, on the 1990s.

In the referendums of April 1993, the electorate decided that the use of PR should be vastly reduced in elections to the Senate. However, it was understood that a vote for the reform of the electoral rules for the Senate was in fact a vote for wider change, as the referendum question was limited to the Senate for technical reasons (see above). The government of Giuliano Amato resigned and was replaced by a caretaker government, which for the first time included non-MPs in the cabinet. The new government, headed by Carlo Azeglio Ciampi, director of the Bank of Italy, had the specific task of carrying through the reform.

Electoral rules were not written into the 1948 constitution and this made them more amenable to change than the institutions of the constitutional order. Even before the referendum that led to the reform of the parliamentary electoral rules, a new, first-past-the-post electoral system and the direct election of mayors had been brought in for local elections. In August, new electoral rules were approved for both houses of parliament. Under the new rules, 475 of the 630 members of the Chamber of Deputies are elected in single-member constituencies. In this part of the election, the constituency candidate with the largest number of votes in that constituency wins. The remaining 155 seats (one-quarter of the total) are allocated by a system of PR in twenty-six multi-member constituencies. Only parties obtaining at least 4 per cent of the vote in the PR part of the election can be allocated seats.

Voters have two ballot papers. One is used to vote for a constituency candidate and the other is used to vote for a party list. This allows voters, if they wish, to vote for one party in their constituency and another in the party lists. In the competition for the 75 per cent of seats that are elected in the single-member constituencies, parties are forced to cooperate in alliances or blocks to stand a chance of winning the seat. The new system therefore has the effect of forcing the formation of alliances or coalitions to fight the single-member constituency elections and in theory should create pressure for a simplification of the multi-party system and movement towards a two-party system.

Italy's very pure system of PR had been seen as a major cause of the lack of clear lines of governmental accountability. The multi-party system led inevitably to bargaining among the parties, as no one party could impose its choice of office holders or legislative programme on the others. Because of this, the electorate could not judge the parties of power on their individual merits. Multi-partyism was also held responsible for cabinet instability and the long-term domination of politics by the DC. Ultimately, then, the system of PR was perceived by many as deeply implicated in rule by the parties and political corruption.

Whether or not the electoral reform is a remedy for Italy's ills will not be clear for some time. The electoral reform will probably take several electoral cycles to settle in, as parties adjust to its implications for organisation and strategy in the electoral competition. In the meantime, reforms of the constitution itself are being prepared.

Constitutional reform: the 'presidentialist' project

There have long been complaints, especially from the right of Italian politics, that Italy is 'ungovernable'. In this view, parliament is over-powerful and the opposition (which until the 1990s effectively meant the PCI) has too much power to thwart government plans and prevent the executive from pursuing a coherent course: the elected government should be allowed to govern and Italy's wide array of liberal institutions are a deterrent to effective decision-making. One of the most important strands of this sort of thinking held the Gaullist-inspired Fifth Republic of France as a model for constitutional reform. General de Gaulle abhorred the excessive powers of the French National Assembly. The 1958 constitution, drawn up in accordance with his preferences, was intended to locate authority primarily in the person of the President, the office he himself would assume, and subordinate prime ministers and their cabinets to decisions emanating from the presidential palace. In an amendment of 1962, the President was to be directly elected by the people. Direct election conferred on the office the authority of popular mandate and intensified the personal relationship between the head of State and the people.

The analogies between the Fourth Republic of France and the fractious multi-partyism of Italy made de Gaulle's solution an obvious template for Italian constitutional reform. Outside the extreme right, the presidentialist project in Italy was most famously associated with Francesco Cossiga (President of the Republic 1985–92), and Bettino Craxi (leader of the PSI and the first Socialist Prime Minister, 1983–7). Cossiga often used the charisma of the Presidency as a platform for his views, especially on the excessive power of the parties. Craxi's premiership seemed for a while to put institutional reform in a presidential direction firmly on the political agenda. But Craxi and the PSI were not able to overtake the PCI to become the main party of the left. The PSI – which by this time had lost any meaningful claim to being socialist – remained the much smaller party and, although an important party of government, it did not gain decisive influence over the political agenda. Craxi himself was later disgraced in the corruption scandals.

The theme of executive empowerment again emerged strongly during the brief premiership of Silvio Berlusconi in 1994. The story of Berlusconi's battles with the power-dispersing institutions of the 1948 constitution is recounted in chapter 8.

The left's alternative to the project of presidentialism, with its sometimes despotic undertones, has been far less clear. Historically, the PCI was defensive and even proud of the liberal constitution it had helped to forge. But as the corruption scandals emerged to rock Italy in the early 1990s, it became easy to confuse defence of the old institutions with a defence of the corrupt old order. Increasingly, a popular will for accountable, efficient and clean government has been perceived to converge with a call for reform along the lines proposed from the right. As a result, the leadership of the main party of the left has become deeply ambiguous on the issue and the case for restraining the executive in a politically fragmented society has not been made clear.

Despite the domination of the debate by the language of the right, a presidential system involving a massive concentration of powers in the office of a directly elected President seems unlikely in Italy. Even de Gaulle was unable to impose such a system in its purest form, and presidentialism in France is increasingly tempered, for example by frequent periods of 'cohabitation' when the Prime Minister and President are from different parties and decisions must be shared and negotiated between the two offices. What is more, Italy in the 1990s is not France in the 1950s. De Gaulle brought in his constitutional project in the context not only of internal political blockage but of massive internal and external crisis in the form of the Algerian war. He was greeted as a hero by the people and had a very free hand in the resolution of the crisis. Constitutional reform in Italy is taking place under very different circumstances. It cannot be imposed by a single 'author' mandated to lead at a time of crisis and the reform package will have to be negotiated among the various parties.

The special procedures of constitutional reform

In Italy, constitutional reform is a special case of legislation. Constitutional changes have to be passed with a two-thirds majority in both houses of parliament, or they may be submitted to the people in the form of a referendum. Part of the underlying philosophy of the constitution is that it should not be readily changed. The constitution lays down the rules that govern the relationships between the political decision-makers and the people and places formal constraints on what the executive can decide and how the decisions are to be made. It has therefore been put out of reach of the executive it is there to restrain. It is not possible, in other words, for government to change the rules of the game without the support of a good part of the opposition. This contrasts with the more ancient democracy of the UK, in which the constitution, which is not written as a single document, may be changed by ordinary law. Because of the special rules governing constitutional amendment in Italy, before the establishment in 1997 of the bicameral reform commission, alterations to the constitution had been rare and limited to rather minor areas.

The bicameral commission of 1997

The left-of-centre government headed by Romano Prodi assumed the extensive reform of constitutional arrangements as one of its central tasks. A bicameral commission was established on 22 January 1997 to draft proposals for change. The commission comprised thirty-five deputies and thirty-five senators, who were nominated by the presidents of the two houses on the advice of the parliamentary parties. The composition of the commission thus reflects the proportions of the different political groupings in parliament. Its task is to draft a reform of part two of the constitution, which governs relations between the different branches of the State. Four main areas of reform have been discussed in three subcommittees. These are:

1 *The form of the State.* Here the debate focused on proposals for further devolution towards a federal State.
2 *The form of government and bicameralism.* This subcommittee was concerned especially with the relations between the executive and parliament.
3 *The system of guarantees.* The emphasis here was on the powers and independence of the judiciary.

The bicameral commission also discussed proposals for further changes in the electoral system.

The bicameral commission reported in summer 1997 after six months of deliberation. Its proposals are outlined below. However, it should be remembered that they may undergo considerable alteration during the process of ratification in parliament.

1 *The form of the State.* The commission has made rather timid proposals for increased taxing and spending powers for the regions. The Northern League is unlikely to be satisfied by the degree of devolution involved.
2 *The form of government.* The commission recommends the direct election of the President. However, the commission does not propose that this office be equipped with a full array of executive powers, although it will clearly have a much enlarged role, for example in foreign and defence

policy. As before, the President must appoint a Prime
Minister from the largest party or coalition. Such an arrangement, if retained, is likely to result in periods of
cohabitation. The commission has also proposed a reduction in the size of parliament. Under the commission's
proposals, seats in the Chamber of Deputies would be
reduced from 630 to 400, and in the Senate from 315 to
200. A smaller, third chamber would be added to give
specific representation to the regions.

3 *Judicial reform*. This has been deferred and must be debated
in full parliament.

4 *Electoral reform*. The committee proposes the retention of
the present 75 per cent to 25 per cent mix of first past the
post and PR. However, a 'bonus' of seats would be allocated
to the coalition winning the most votes.

The commission's proposals must be returned to parliament
and in some cases submitted to referendum. Even in the absence of major crises such as the fall of government, the
process of ratifying the reforms is unlikely to be completed
before 1998.

Further reading

Hine, D. *Governing Italy: The Politics of Bargained Pluralism*, Oxford
(1993).

Hine, D. and Finocchi, R. 'The Italian Prime Minister', *West European
Politics*, Vol. 14, No. 2 (1991).

For the 1993 electoral reform see Lo Verso, L. and McLean, I. 'The Italian
General Election of March 1994', *Electoral Studies*, Vol. 14, No. 1
(March 1995).

3

The regions

A country of contrasts

Rarely does one medium-sized country such as Italy offer such a range of tradition and experience. There is diversity in geographical and climatic conditions – from the mountain villages of the Alps to the blazing, arid plains of Calabria. There is diversity in economic conditions – from the trend-setting Milanese middle class to the wretched conditions of Naples' urban poor. Often, local dialects are preferred to 'classic' Italian, although the latter is insisted on in the schools. These dialects are often incomprehensible to those who know only the national language. Everywhere, there is intense pride in local achievements, traditions, products and cuisine. This pride itself has a specific name in Italian – *campanilismo* – a word derived from the *campanile*, or church tower, that stands over each local community. Pride and identification in locality, and an accompanying sense of rivalry with neighbouring areas, are often even today more important than national patriotism in defining the identity of the Italian citizen.

Regional identity in Italy

Despite this, territorially based ethnic or linguistic cleavages do not have great political significance in Italy. Separatist movements or tendencies have existed and do exist in, for example, the islands of Sicily and Sardinia, the Val d'Aosta, with its French-speaking inhabitants, and especially the Alto Adige, the former South Tyrol, with its large German-speaking minority. However, these movements have not constituted the threat to State survival given, for example, by nationalist movements in the Basque Country or Ireland. Separatist sentiments in these regions were accommodated to some extent by the granting of special status and greater autonomy at the foundation of the Republic, after the Second World War. A fifth 'special region', Friuli-Venezia Giulia, was created later.

With the exception of these peripheral areas, in which geographical and linguistic factors gave rise to particularly intense separate cultural identities, the demand for independent political representation of territorial units has not been strong through most of the life of the Republic. In part, this was because localist sentiment in Italy was identified more closely with cities and inter-city rivalry than with regions. Many of the northern and central regions did have some historical identity: the regions of Piedmont, Liguria, Lombardy, the Veneto and Tuscany correspond, though rather roughly, to the territorial States of the sixteenth and seventeenth centuries. However, these regions were in most cases shaped by the great cities that dominated them, undermining potential demands for representation in the national legislature and independent powers for the region as a whole.

More recently, such a demand has been voiced by the Northern League, a populist and federalist movement based largely on small-business interests, whose electoral support rose rapidly in the north in the early 1990s. The leadership of this movement proposed the division of Italy into three 'macro-regions': 'Padania' in the north, 'Etruria' in the centre, and – rather more prosaically – 'the South'. However, despite attempts by the leadership to furnish Padania with a set of symbols and ceremonies (flags, a capital, a parliament and even a sort of standing army with its own uniform), this new regional party is not bound by a genuinely common cultural heritage, or by special demands for the redress of ancient wrongs. Its appeal was rather founded on disgust over the corruption of the traditional parties of the middle class, a perception that this corruption is connected to the 'southernisation' of the State bureaucracy and the main parties of coalition, and resentment over the use in the south of resources generated in the prosperous north. Although the party's attempts to engineer a cultural identity to unite the north appear as rather farcical, it has undoubtedly been an important force in creating a consensus around the need for increased regional independence.

The south

The most glaringly obvious of territorial divides in Italy is that which separates the prosperous north from the less favoured south.

The causes of southern underdevelopment have long been debated and a variety of factors have been implicated, in various combinations. These include: the long period of foreign domination by the Bourbons; the lack of natural resources; inaccessibility and geographical distance from 'modern' Europe; lingering residues of feudal relations that for a long time prevented the emergence of commercial farming; the emergence and persistence of the Mafia, which seemed to blight any hope of indigenous legal enterprise; the persistence of a culture of dependency on the central State; and the continual drain of enterprising individuals through emigration.

As in the north, there is no one, common southern culture: there is as much economic, cultural and linguistic diversity within the south as between south and north. Although there is little cultural basis for a 'southern' identity, it might be thought that the extreme disadvantage that has been the south's lot since before unification, coupled with the perception that the economic progress of the north was gained at the expense of continued southern deprivation, could have united the south in common cause and given rise to demands for autonomy. Many scholars of the southern question have implicated the actions of the central State in the continued privation of the south. However, the central State in Italy has also been a source of immediate economic succour in the south, providing jobs and benefits for those unable to secure their own subsistence. Enormous sums of money have been injected into the south through the mediation of the central State, most notably in the form of the Fund for the South.

The southern riots of 1969–73, and especially the riots of Reggio in Calabria in 1970, are emblematic of the degree of material dependence of the south on the State and the consequent barriers to the emergence of a southern identity and demands for regional independence.

As we will see below, 1970 saw the long-delayed implementation of the regional assemblies foreseen by the constitution. The inhabitants of Reggio had secured promises that their town would be the new regional capital. In the summer of 1970, however, it was announced that the capital would, after all, be located in Catanzaro, on the opposite coast of Calabria. Protests at the decision were organised first by the DC ex-mayor, but later escalated, under the leadership of the neo-Fascists, into a violent revolt. The disorders continued for more than a year. The railway station, post office, airport and local television station were all occupied at various times, and the prefecture and police headquarters were attacked. However, the riots were very far from an expression of injured regional pride. The location of the regional capital elsewhere would have deprived Reggio of hundreds of clerical and administrative jobs. In an area of spectacularly high unemployment, this was tremendously important. Tensions in Reggio were ultimately eased by the location there of the regional assembly (though not the capital) and the announcement of plans to build a vast new steelworks at nearby Gioia Tauro. The steelworks – begun at a time when the European steel industry was already in difficulties – was never built, although a major port was constructed where acres of citrus and olive groves had once stood.

This episode illustrates the way in which the central State has attempted to maintain public order in the poorest regions of the south through the preferential allocation of public works that in many cases are primarily 'make-work' projects, ill-attuned to the needs of the local, or national, economy. For the people of the south, in turn, there is good reason to fear any devolution of power to the local level which might imply cutting the vital lifeline from the central State. Such a rationale goes a long way to explain the south's high vote for the DC in the long period of their domination and the tendency, after the collapse of the old party system in 1993, to switch allegiance from the DC to the right-wing Italian Social Movement (Movimento Sociale Italiano, MSI) (later to become the National Alliance), whose nationalist ideology pits it against proposals for more federal arrangements in Italy.

A history of centralisation

Until relatively recent times, local government has played a comparatively small part in the Italian political system. From the beginning of Italy's existence as a unified country, the Italian State was highly centralised. Italy's strong tradition of central government was in large part a reaction to the centrifugal threat posed by the geographical, socio-economic and linguistic diversity described above.

Some political elites in the period of unification favoured the idea of a more federal arrangement that could have accommodated local sentiments by allowing a degree of self-government. But for others, a centralised and unitary State was seen as essential if the new regime was to replace the old sources of authority and exert its power over the country as a whole, to forge a new era of national prosperity. It was feared, in other words, that granting real powers to local governments or authorities would undermine the fragile unity of a nation

State that had been superimposed, largely by main force, on the collection of heterogeneous communities it was attempting to replace.

Fears of the strain that the devolution of power would place on the unity of the new State led to the promulgation of the Ricasoli law of 1861, which extended the centralised and uniform Piedmontese administrative structure to whole of the new Kingdom of Italy. Bettino Ricasoli, Prime Minister from June 1861, was an admirer of the system of government put in place by Napoleon III. In line with this model, powerful prefects were assigned by central government to control, often in minute detail, the budgets and activities of local government.

But despite the high degree of formal centralisation of the new State, it was apparent that the goodwill and cooperation of local elites would be necessary if centrally decided policy was to be enacted effectively on the ground. From the start, there existed an informal system of accommodation and compromise with local notables. The prefects were open to negotiation at local level and local interests could also appeal to the central State through local deputies.

The formal powers of local government were increased somewhat after the First World War. War mobilisation and the growth of industrialisation had led to a multiplication of the administrative tasks the central State had to carry out, adding to the pressure for some devolution. In addition, the new territories of Trentino-Alto Adige and Friuli-Venezia Giulia had been absorbed into Italy and would have been reluctant to give up the degree of autonomy they had enjoyed under Austrian rule. For the brief period before the advent of Fascism, local government experienced a degree of independence.

Centralisation and the Fascist legacy

The centralisation of the Italian political system was reinforced during the period of Fascism. As in other forms of right-wing authoritarianism, an exacerbated national pride and patriotism was a key element in the ideology of Fascism. The Fascist propagandists set about the creation of a homogeneous and totalitarian culture through the schools, media and party organisations. However, they were little more successful in this project of 'making Italians' than were the leaders of the liberal regime, creating, rather, a passive consensus based on the fear of reprisal for any expression of dissent. The Fascist State was never able totally to suppress difference and pluralism.

The impact of Fascism was more enduring in terms of its legacy on institutional arrangements. No other source of authority could be allowed to compete openly with that of the leader, to whom unquestioning obedience was demanded. One of the various measures taken to cement the dictatorship in the mid-1920s was the abolition of elected local governments and their replacement by appointed officials. When elected local government was restored after the fall of Fascism, it had been weakened by the long interlude.

The regions in the constitution

After the Second World War, the abolition of the monarchy and the election of the Constituent Assembly gave Italy the chance to draw up a constitution that could truly reflect the social and political make-up of its people and embark on a democratic and inclusive course, in marked contrast to the narrow base of politics of the liberal era and the authoritarian rule of Fascism. And as we have seen, the document drawn up by the Constituent Assembly, which was made up of all the main anti-Fascist forces in society, did appear on paper as a highly progressive framework for the emergent democracy.

The first constitution of the Italian Republic, adopted in 1948, sketched out a framework for a new political system that, among other things, was to give considerable powers to elected regional assemblies. These provisions were largely in reaction to the centralised authoritarianism of Fascism and were, at first, strongly favoured by the DC. The concept of subsidiarity – the devolution of power as near as possible to the people – was after all Catholic in origin.

In the immediate post-war period the PCI opposed decentralisation. Its leadership saw a strong central executive as essential to guide the country through the profound socio-economic change it hoped to force through. Until 1947, the PCI participated in government and even after its summary ejection from power it retained the strategic goal of governing in alliance with the progressive elements of the DC and implementing a programme of radical social reform. However, by 1948 the DC had altered its position. Presciently, the party feared that power in elected regional assemblies might fall into the hands of the left-wing opposition, especially in the so-called red areas of central Italy. For the same reason, the left also reversed its traditional ideology of centralisation. Given the historical conditions, the capture of the central State and the chance to wield its full powers was not an option in the short term. A trend to regional autonomy and the chance to win power at a local level was therefore in the interests of the opposition. But, as we saw in chapter 2, the DC was able to consolidate its position of domination of the Italian political system and from this position it was able to prevent the implementation of the constitutional provisions for the devolution of power until 1970, a full twenty-two years after the adoption of the constitution. Exceptions to this were the five 'special regions', mentioned above.

The DC was aided in its resistance to the constitutional requirement for regional structures by the hostility of the bureaucracy to any form of devolution. In a tradition continued by the DC, Mussolini and the Fascist National Party had used the offer of jobs in the public administration as a source of patronage to bolster support for the regime, especially among the lower middle classes. After the fall of Fascism, it was practically impossible, and politically unwise, to renew the bureaucracy, despite its strong taint of Fascism. The

Roman bureaucracy could be counted upon to resist any progress towards increasing the powers of local authorities at the expense of its own.

The importance of local politics

Although the structure of the Italian State was centralised until at least the 1970s, local politics was very important in Italy and was taken more seriously than in the UK, which also has a centralised, unitary system. The very high levels of interest in local politics and the high visibility of important local politicians, such as the mayors of the large cities, are understandable in the context of the strong allegiance to locality, or *campanilismo*, outlined above. Although increasing geographical mobility, expanded access to education, the development of national media and improved transport and communication systems may be gradually eroding local differences, the legacy of late unification and late industrialisation is still felt in a profound attachment to the town or even village of origin.

In Italy, as elsewhere, a post in local government is the most obvious springboard for a career in national politics and a strong local following is obviously an advantage for future advancement. But this local factor was amplified in Italy by the mechanisms of the national electoral system. Under the Italian system of PR, reformed in 1993, constituency candidates did not automatically benefit from votes for their party cast in their constituency, as in the UK. Voters voted for a party list and parliamentary seats were allocated on the basis of the proportion of votes for each party. The higher a candidate was ranked on the list, the greater was his or her chance of election to parliament. In addition to this, the Italian system allowed voters to indicate their order of preference for individual candidates on the list, thus increasing their chances of election. The 'packet' of personal votes a politician could demonstrate was vital not only for election but for her or his career in the party. Politicians who were able to secure grants, public works projects, special legislation or other benefits for the people of their area – thus boosting their preference votes – would have a much enhanced chance of progress in the party at national level. Thus PR and especially the preference vote system – which was abolished following a referendum in 1991 – provided extra inducement to politicians of all ranks to remain highly attentive to their local bases of support.

The establishment of the regions

As we will see in the next chapter, the DC domination of the Italian political system came increasingly under threat through the 1960s and 1970s. The vote for the PCI was gradually rising, narrowing the DC's room for manoeuvre and threatening the coalitions it dominated. This process led first to the so-called opening to the left in the early 1960s, in which the PSI was brought into coalition, and then, in 1976, to the first government of national unity, in which the PCI was offered non-ministerial posts in return for its support of the government. As the power of the DC declined, so too did its capacity to resist the enablement of the constitutional provisions for the creation of regional assemblies.

Both parties of the left were committed to regionalisation, not least because of the promise of local power implicit for the left in such reform. The PSI made the establishment of regional assemblies one of the conditions for its support for the governing coalition of 1962 and for its entrance into the coalition from December 1963. However, the pact fell through, as powerful right-wing elements within the DC balked at the prospect of Communist-led regional governments. Regional devolution, along with other reforms, was quietly shelved. The promise of structural reforms that seemed to be proffered by the opening to the left was dashed and the resulting sense of frustration contributed to a rising tide of working-class and youth protest in the late 1960s and early 1970s.

The regionalist front was given further impetus by the protests of the new left, as the devolution of power to the localities seemed in tune with a new mood stressing popular participation in politics and the more active engagement of citizens in political decision-making. The laws enabling the establishment of the regional assemblies were finally passed in 1970.

The structure, financing and powers of regional government

The reality of regional reform fell well short of satisfying more ambitious expectations, especially in the early phases. Like many of the other reforms of this period, regionalism was better on paper than in practice. Conservative national politicians and the central administration joined forces to impose restraints on the powers and resources of the new regional assemblies.

Structure

The 1970 reform added the regions as a third tier of local government in Italy, superimposing fifteen ordinary regions over the already existing provinces, based on the ninety-five leading towns and their surrounding areas, and municipalities, or *comuni*. The five special regions were already in place.

Each region elects an assembly, or council, of thirty to eighty members, depending on its population size. Regional elections are held every five years. Elections were by PR until 1993 when electoral reform, in line with the reform of the national electoral rules, gave the largest party a bonus of seats, designed to discourage coalition government. The assembly elects its executive, known as the *giunta*, and a regional president. The regional government is divided into departments, or *assessorati*, mirroring the ministerial structure of central government.

Financing

The regional assemblies have little financial autonomy and are heavily reliant on central government for funding in the form of grants or transfers. Furthermore, the regions enjoyed little discretion in their use of these central government grants, much of which comes earmarked for specific purposes. Thus the regions are very restricted in their ability to develop and implement coherent local policies, and their function is largely to administer the policies developed by central government.

The funding of the regions by central government followed a formula favouring the less advantaged regions, contributing to the redistribution of resources from the north to the south.

Powers

The legislative powers of the regional assemblies are similarly limited and there is, furthermore, considerable confusion about the respective powers of centre and region. About one-quarter of laws passed by the regions in their first legislature were vetoed by the centre.

The constitution specified a number of policy areas in which the regions could legislate, although regional legislation had to remain 'within the limits of the fundamental principles established by the laws of the State' (article 117). In other words, it had to be compatible with national law. The areas specified by the constitution have in many cases been overtaken by events. For example, the power to legislate in the domain of 'public charities, health and hospital assistance' has been superseded by the local administration of the National Health Service. However, the addition of 'other matters indicated by constitutional laws' to the seventeen policy areas specified in the constitution did give some flexibility to update regional powers in line with developments.

The increasing powers of the regions in the 1970s

The PCI had clear interests in pressing for the devolution of further powers and finance to the regions. In the first regional elections, of June 1970, the PCI had, predictably, captured power in the 'red' regions of Emilia-Romagna, Tuscany and Umbria. In the second regional elections, of June 1975, the PCI increased its vote by 6.5 per cent and, with the support of the PSI, was able to establish left-wing *giuntas* in Lombardy, Piedmont and Liguria as well.

By the mid-1970s, the DC needed to hold out an olive branch to the PCI. Electoral support for the DC was gradually eroding, while the PCI was experiencing an upsurge that peaked in 1976, when it gained more than one-third of the vote for the first time (see figure 4.1, p. 64). The resulting influx of Communist MPs into parliament altered the delicately balanced mathematics of the governing coalition and PCI support – or at least abstention – had become more important for government stability. One of the compromises on offer in order to secure this support was increased financing and empowerment of regions.

In 1977, important new powers were given to the regions. Reforms of the way taxes were distributed gave the regions responsibility for about one-quarter of the national budget, improving their ability to plan ahead in their activities. However, regional funds still largely emanated from the centre and the regions' own resources remained small. New tasks were also devolved to regional level. The most important among these was responsibility for hospitals and the health-care system. The regions' spheres of legislative authority now included health, housing, urban planning, agriculture, public works and vocational training. Importantly, though, the centre retained the power to veto regional legislation.

The 1977 reform also gave the regional assemblies a voice in the formulation of national policy. A variety of consultative committees were set up in different sectors of policy-making and these have acted as important forums through which the regions are able to make their influence felt in national decision-making.

Although these innovations increased the powers of the regions, partially reversing the one-way, top-down flow of decision-making, they did nothing to clarify the vexed problem of the respective competencies of central and local government. Disputes about what the different levels of government can and cannot do are frequent and the Constitutional Court is often called in to settle them.

All in all, although the reforms of the 1970s moved Italy some way towards the decentralisation of power, the degree of devolution obtained was in no way comparable to that obtaining in federal states such as Germany or the USA.

The performance of the regions

Even after these reforms, the regions in reality fell well short of the hopes in some quarters that they would offer a new dimension of bottom-up, participatory politics and local governance that could countermand DC rule from the centre. Regional governments were staffed mainly by bureaucrats transferred from the centre and even when recruitment was left to the regional authorities themselves it often followed old patterns, in which jobs were shared out on the basis of party-political allegiance rather than qualification and experience. The regions' administration of the new National Health Service has come in for particular criticism in this regard.

However, the performance of the regions, and their popularity among citizens, has varied very widely from case to case. Regional government appears to have been particularly efficient in the case of *giuntas* outside of the old ruling coalition, although performance in some regions with a traditionally 'white' (DC) government, notably the Veneto, has also been good. In a major study of regional performance in Italy, Robert Putnam and his colleagues (see further reading) found that performance on a range of criteria tended to be better in the

'red' *giuntas* of central Italy. The authors link this phenomenon more to traditions of cooperation and mutual trust in
these regions than to the capacities of the Communists per se,
although the PCI's relative exclusion from the increasingly
corrupt spoils-sharing system described in the next chapter, as
well as its desire to prove itself ready for the mantle of central
power, are also plausible factors in an explanation.

Regional government and the 'third Italy'

A vast body of literature has been dedicated to the strong
economic performance of the so-called 'third Italy', dis-
tinguished from the large-scale industrial structure of the
north-west and the 'backward' south by its thriving small-scale
but technologically advanced industries. Much of this literature emphasises the role of 'clean', more innovative and efficient
regional authorities which have nurtured high-technology,
high-skill enterprises and encouraged them to coordinate and
share resources. The central Italian region of Emilia-Romagna,
with its 'red' *giunta*, has received particular attention. According to this literature, innovative entrepreneurs, trade unions
and regional governments, bound together by common sets of
political ideas, were able to cooperate to establish local associations and institutions that could help small capital survive in
big capital's world. Regional governments in Emilia-Romagna
and elsewhere in central Italy have been able to help entrepreneurs to create associations which provide administrative
services, coordinate purchasing, carry out market research for
associated firms and provide facilities for computer-aided de-
sign and so on. They have also helped in the establishment of
cooperatives, providing guarantees for bank loans at low rates
of interest. Such services, it is argued, have been instrumental
in allowing small and medium-sized local enterprises to suc-
ceed in the face of competition from the multi-national giants.

  While other literature points out the limitations of this
model, it is undoubtedly true that the economies of these

regions have proved more resilient than others in times of national economic downturn and have performed well according to most economic measures (for example, rate of unemployment, rate of growth of money income per head, share of exports).

The prospects for further devolution

As the previous chapter showed, some further devolution of powers to the regions seems likely, although its extent will not be known until the constitutional reforms currently under discussion are ratified. The bicameral commission set up to review the constitution has suggested the establishment of a small third chamber of representatives chosen from the regions. This was (for the moment) preferred to the more radical proposal of converting the upper house (Senate) into a chamber of regional representation, rather like the German Bundesrat.

The degree of devolution or federalisation that Italy chooses will be the outcome of compromise. Much will depend on the balance of power in the debate held by the Northern League, which will not be happy with any reform that does not allow the regions to retain the lion's share of the proceeds of taxation for their own use. But opposition to such a reform will be strong, especially among representatives with large constituencies in the south, as the poorer southern regions would stand to lose an important mechanism by which, under current arrangements, revenues from general taxation are shifted from north to south.

Further reading

Cassese, S. and Torchia, L. 'The Meso Level in Italy', in Sharpe, L. J. (ed.), *The Rise of Meso Government in Europe*, London (1993).

Levy, C. (ed.) *Italian Regionalism: History, Identity and Politics*, Oxford (1996).

Putnam, R., *et al. Making Democracy Work: Civic Traditions in Modern Italy*, Princeton (1993).

4

The regime of the parties

Introduction

From shortly after the Second World War until the collapse of the party system following the corruption scandals of the early 1990s, Italy was governed by a series of coalitions dominated by the DC.

Until the early 1960s, the coalitions were made up from the DC and the small secular parties such as the Liberals, Republicans and Social Democrats. From 1962–3 the potential parties of government were extended to include the PSI. The PCI, however, was excluded from power (with the brief exception of 1976–9) even though it consistently gained up to one-third of the vote. Because of the DC's long-lasting stranglehold over power, and the exclusion of the main party of opposition, Italy has sometimes been called a blocked democracy.

The DC, however, never ruled alone. The political, administrative and economic power-holding positions were shared out among the governing parties, and although the DC was usually able to keep a hold on the posts it was most interested in, it was obliged to distribute the spoils of government increasingly widely. This was, until 1976, because the PCI's proportion of the vote was tending to increase (see figure 4.1), making the DC increasingly reliant on the parliamentary support of other parties. Collusion and spoils-sharing among the parties increasingly became the hallmark of government in Italy, until the distinction between legal and illegal became blurred and

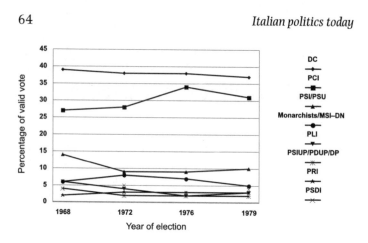

Figure 4.1   *Elections to the Chamber of Deputies, 1968–79*

the whole system collapsed under the weight of its own corruption.

What is Christian Democracy?

The DC was founded in 1942 from the remnants of Don
Sturzo's PPI that had survived Fascism. The party leader,
Alcide De Gasperi, was both anti-Fascist and anti-Communist,
and from the start was determined to steer a course for the DC
that would be independent from the conservatism of the Vatican and from the radicalism of the party's left wing. Unlike the
PPI, the new Catholic party was soon able to enjoy the consistent support of the Vatican, as the Church became increasingly
worried by the strength of the left and the popularity it was
gaining from its active role in the Resistance movement. The
Church therefore overcame any misgivings about involvement
in secular politics and swung its considerable resources behind
the new party.

The social bases and *raison d'être* of the new Catholic party
were basically the same as those of its predecessor. Like the

PPI, it did not claim to represent the interests of a particular class or section of society. The adoption of the name Christian Democracy was a signal that it was not to be a confessional party of the Catholic faithful, but would seek to represent all segments of Italian society.

Unlike many conservative parties elsewhere in Europe, therefore, the DC did not emerge as the main party representing business interests, although private industry was influential on it. However, many leaders of large-scale private industry tended to support one or other of the smaller, 'lay' parties, usually the Republicans (Partito Repubblicano Italiano, PRI) or Liberals (Partito Liberale Italiano, PLI). Because of this, the DC did not develop a distinctively pro-business ideology favouring the interests of modern management. Its identity was not founded in the representation of a particular socio-economic grouping in society, such as class, but rather in a generic appeal to anti-Communism and to Catholic and family values. The cornerstones of the DC's electoral support were farmers, especially the poor peasants of the south, and the very large sector of small businesses and the self-employed, but it also presented itself as the party of the Catholic working class.

Factionalism

The DC was gradually permeated by the very wide range of societal interests it was attempting to represent. This permeability opened the party to factionalisation, as groupings within it jostled for privileged access to the positions of power that would allow them to further the concerns of the particular interests that backed them.

The first faction emerged in the early 1950s, around the personality of Amintore Fanfani, who was party secretary from 1954 to 1959. Like De Gasperi, Fanfani wanted to reduce the party's dependence on the Church and on private industry, and to build and consolidate the party's membership. It was during the years of his rising influence, in the 1950s, that the DC established its power base in the State-controlled industries and banks. The State sector was a rich source of the patronage – or distribution of largesse – that became so important in sustaining the electoral popularity of the party. However, Fanfani's pragmatic support for an alliance with the PSI made him powerful enemies especially among the party's right wing. In 1959 the government he led fell and he resigned his post as party secretary.

Factionalism within the DC increased after Fanfani's fall from dominance. In 1959, a group of men, many of whom were former members of Fanfani's own faction, met in the convent of S. Dorotea. The new faction, the Dorotei, was to dominate the party through the 1960s. The highly conservative Dorotei were opposed to the opening to the left and contributed to the difficulties experienced by the centre-left governments from 1963 and their failure to implement meaningful reform.

After the mid-1970s, no one faction was able to dominate the party and endow it with a coherent leadership. The amorphous nature of the leadership contributed to the increasing difficulties the party experienced in maintaining its domination of the Italian political system.

The DC's rise to power

Catholic 'associationism'

As we have seen, Mussolini and the Fascist regime had attempted to uproot the independent parties, trade unions and voluntary associations that might have formed the basis of opposition to his regime. Because of this, the Republic was born in a sort of associational vacuum, in which the civic institutions and associations that are the stuff of modern democracies were largely absent. However, there was one general exception to this. Mussolini realised he would not be able to combat the power and appeal of the Catholic Church and instead chose to accommodate with it. The Church was therefore allowed to retain considerable control over education and a wealth of charitable and welfare institutions. The Catholic Church and the DC thus had a flying start in the creation of the web of associations that underpinned the competing Christian Democratic and Communist subcultures in post-war Italy. The DC emerged after the war ready supplied with an army of experienced and influential activists in the lay organisation, Catholic Action, which coordinates the Church's social, political and professional organisations. The party's leadership was drawn largely from the Catholic Graduate Association. Other important associations were quickly built, such as the Christian Associations of Italian Workers (Associazioni Cristiane dei Lavoratori Italiani, ACLI) and the Association of Peasant Proprietors (Coldiretti), both of which offered insurance and welfare assistance. These associations were invaluable in rooting support for the DC and combating the spread of Communism among the population.

The Cold War

The DC's rise to power was facilitated by the conditions of Cold War gripping Europe following the end of the Second World War. The USA, in its emerging role as the dominant world power, was deeply anxious about the threat to liberal democracy and open markets posed by Communism. Italy stands at the European frontier between West and East and, what is more, the PCI emerged at the end of the Second World War as the largest Communist party in the Western world. It is not surprising, then, that Italy was one of the terrains on which the Cold War was fought most bitterly. To those in power in the USA, it appeared that only the DC could stand in the way of Communism in Italy. And so the USA threw its might and wealth behind the DC. Marshall Aid was poured into the Catholic welfare associations and, during the campaign for the 1948 general election, George Marshall warned that US aid to Italy would cease if the PCI were victorious. The message was reinforced with the threat of military intervention. In the weeks running up to the election, for example, US warships were anchored in the main Italian ports.

The match was not an even one. The DC emerged from the 1948 election with 48.5 per cent of the vote and an absolute majority in the Chamber of Deputies. The Popular Front, combining Communists and Socialists, gained 31 per cent, a drop of nearly nine percentage points from the total obtained by the left parties in 1946.

The party system

The ideological diversity that had characterised Italy in the liberal era had not been eradicated during the Fascist regime, merely suppressed. It is therefore not surprising that as political life recommenced after the war, a variety of parties developed to press the interests of their constituencies on the State and bring their concerns to the attention of the public at large.

On the left, the PCI emerged in the post-war period as the leading party of the working class. It was particularly strong in the central regions and among the industrial workers of the north-west. The PSI, weakened by the split off of the Social Democratic Party in 1947, was increasingly pushed into the shadow of its big brother.

The centre of the political space was occupied not only by the DC, but also by the small liberal and lay parties which emerged or re-emerged in the immediate post-war period as an inheritance of the liberal and secular forces of unification. These parties were the Republicans, the Liberals and the Social Democrats. The Republicans, in particular, had the support of some of the country's leading industrialists, including that of Gianni Agnelli, owner of the car giant FIAT.

On the right was a small, but politically significant, neo-Fascist party, which was formed from the remnants of the German-occupied Italian Social Republic of Salò, from which it took its name, the Movimento Italiano Sociale. The MSI attracted around 5–7 per cent of the vote through most of the post-war period until the collapse of the party system.

The multi-party nature of the emerging political system of the Republic was reinforced by the adoption, from the earliest elections, of its system of PR (see chapter 2). This exacerbated the extreme fragmentation of the party system by encouraging the persistence of very small parties. The system also facilitated the emergence of new parties, especially as youth and protest movements emerged strongly from around the late 1960s. Entrants into the Italian party system from that time were 'new left' parties, the Radical Party and the Greens.

Particracy

The term particracy is used by some political scientists to describe the government of the Italian Republic, at least until the collapse of the traditional parties of power in 1993. Partitocracy, deriving from the Italian *partito* (party), and its Italian translation *partitocrazia* are also used, although they seem to imply the Italian case specifically, rather than a concept which may have more general application.

A particracy is a form of government in which influential personages within the political parties, rather than an executive accountable to parliament, are the primary basis of rule, determining the use of public resources, the allocation of important posts and ultimately the development of policy. Real power resides in the faction leaders and party bosses, who negotiate among themselves to distribute the positions of power, from government office (such as ministerial posts) to key positions of control in the public sector.

As we saw in chapter 2, the Italian constitution gives the power of selecting the Prime Minister to the President of the Republic, but in reality the office holder is chosen through a process of negotiation between powerful politicians of the coalition parties. Once in place, the Prime Minister is unable to select the ministers who will make up the cabinet, but must defer to the outcome of further inter- and intra-party bargaining.

The party notables who wield so much influence do not necessarily hold high office in government. Their power comes not from office, but from the following they can muster among rank-and-file parliamentarians. A loyal following in parliament gives considerable blackmail power in the Italian context, as a government can often be destabilised if a few MPs withdraw their support for it.

The power of the parties

In a multi-party system such as Italy's, it is virtually impossible for the largest party to govern without forming a coalition, or at least negotiating the support of other parties. The DC had an absolute majority in the Chamber of Deputies only in the earliest period of the Republic and even then found it politically prudent to cooperate with other parties.

However, the DC was limited in its choice of potential partners. The PCI was, of course, unacceptable, as the DC's main source of identity was as a bulwark against Communism and, in any case, the USA and the Catholic Church were vehemently opposed to its inclusion in power. The fear of cooperation with the left was such that even the PSI was not considered as a potential coalition partner until 1963.

At the other end of the political spectrum, the neo-Fascist MSI was also considered beyond the democratic pale and was excluded from government. Anti-Fascism was still, understandably, a central pillar of Italian political culture. That a coalition enjoying even the support of the MSI would be intolerable to Italian public opinion of the 'First Republic' was shown by the collapse of the Tambroni government of 1960 (see pp. 93–4).

The exclusion of the PCI, MSI and, until 1962–3, PSI from government made the governing coalitions highly vulnerable. Since large numbers of MPs were neither in the governing coalition nor necessarily supporting it, the desertion to the opposition of even a handful of parliamentarians could lead to a government crisis, in which the governing coalition could no longer secure a majority in parliament. The threat to jump ship did not, of course, have to be carried through: its mere existence was enough to strengthen the hand of the party notables in the perpetual backstage negotiations that have characterised Italian governments.

The power of the party bosses and faction leaders increased as the governing coalition's potential parliamentary support diminished. Relatively minor alterations in Italy's comparatively very stable voting patterns could thus be crucially important.

The economic miracle and changing voting patterns

From about the 1960s, electoral pressure on the DC increased. The main reason for this was the twin processes of secularisation and the declining power of the Church to influence the political choices of the electorate.

The 1950s in Italy had seen what was probably Western Europe's most extraordinary economic miracle. Italy was no longer a backward and predominantly agricultural nation, but had taken its place among the four largest economies of Europe. The effects of this rapid modernisation on the social fabric of Italy were tremendous. The process of industrialisation was accompanied by massive movements from the rural areas to the towns and cities. Transport and communications improved spectacularly and the spread of relatively cheap mass-produced cars such as the FIAT *cinquecento* (500) made holiday and weekend travel affordable for millions of Italian families. Television ownership also increased: televisions, introduced in 1954, were in the homes of nearly one-half of Italian families by 1965. Social mobility was another consequence of the new era, as industrialisation and modernisation led to a growing sector of white-collar workers.

The demand for white-collar work and the increasing need for skills in industry led in turn to the expansion of education. In 1962, secondary education to age fourteen was at last made compulsory.

As Italy catapulted itself into the modern age, millions of Italians moved out from the shadow of the *campanile* – the church bell tower. Numbers regularly attending church declined dramatically, from about two-thirds of the population in the 1950s to about one-half in the early 1970s and a mere one-third in the mid-1980s. The process of secularisation not only tended to erode the DC vote, but also loosened the deeply entrenched 'veto' against voting for the PCI. Although the percentage changes were relatively small, in the context of the tight mathematics of parliament they were very significant. The DC found it increasingly difficult to put together a working coalition. The greater vulnerability of the coalitions was an important factor in the inclusion of the PSI in possible governing formulas from the early 1960s.

Patronage and clientelism

As the DC's room for manoeuvre in coalition negotiations diminished, the party increasingly used the distribution of public resources to bolster its electoral support in a strategy of patronage. Later, other parties began to imitate this strategy, notably the PSI under the leadership of Bettino Craxi from the late 1970s.

An important target of DC patronage was the south, where many people still lived in conditions of imminent poverty, given the backward state of industrial development. Even by the mid-twentieth century, few jobs were available in industry in the south and much of the land was still in the hands of a land-owning class deeply opposed to processes of modernisation that would threaten their prestige. Although some land reform had gradually been enacted, small farmers and labourers were often unable to ensure family survival through their

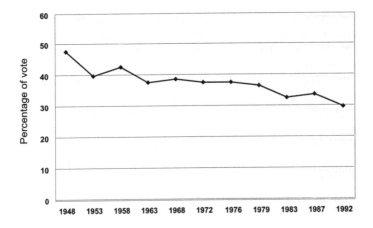

Figure 4.2   *The DC's declining share of valid votes to the Chamber of Deputies, 1948–92*

own resources, and were often dependent on powerful patrons who could wield political influence to secure the jobs and benefits that would alleviate their misery.

Elements among the leadership of the DC, many of whom were themselves southerners in origin, were quick to supply this role in the modern era, using their political influence to secure benefits for their electoral heartland in the south. One common form of patronage was the offer of jobs in the public sector. The predominance of southerners among public officials, from agents of the Carabinieri (the police force under military command) to the civil service and municipal bureaucracies, is still today a visible indicator of the power of patronage. The 'southernisation' of the public administration accelerated as the DC came under increasing electoral pressure from the 1970s (see figure 4.2). Meritocratic criteria for recruitment to the civil service were regularly bypassed by employing candidates on a temporary basis and then legislating to include them in the core workforce. It has been estimated that between 1973 and 1990, some 350,000 people were recruited to temporary jobs in the civil service without entrance examinations and had their posts made permanent by twelve special laws. Some 250,000 persons were recruited according to regular procedures. By the end of this period, between 80 and 90 per cent of high-ranking civil servants were born in the south.

Another example of clientelistic practice was the use of welfare benefits, especially disability pensions. In some cases, eligibility conditions for disability pensions were extended to residency in areas designated as especially economically disadvantaged. The requirement to have a medically certifiable disability was thus removed and those suffering economic deprivation – predominantly in the south – could claim the benefit.

The injection of public finances into major infrastructural and industrial projects was also often used with the clear intent of maintaining electoral support. An important source of finance for this was the fund for the development of the south, the *Cassa per il Mezzogiorno*, over which DC politicians maintained an unbroken line of political control. While many of the projects undertaken in the south were undoubtedly of value, especially in reducing the isolation of the south by developing a modern infrastructure of transport and communication, others were white elephants, whose main purpose was to create jobs.

In this way, the people of the south were shown that a loyal vote for the DC would be rewarded by the allocation of more resources to their locality.

The 'colonisation' of the State and spoils-sharing

The strategies of 'colonisation' and *lottizzazione* (spoils-sharing among the parties) were necessary corollaries to patronage and clientelism. In order to use public resources to bolster votes, the DC needed to control access to them and that meant establishing long-term control over the ministries and departments most influential in the allocation of resources in society.

The top positions in four ministries were 'colonised' by DC politicians almost without interruption throughout the post-war period. These were the Ministries of the Interior, Education, Agriculture, and Posts and Telecommunications. Two other ministries – Foreign Affairs and the Treasury – were colonised almost as thoroughly. As competition among the coalition parties intensified, the DC increasingly needed to obtain the consent of the other governing parties for its continued domination of the chosen ministries. Trade-offs therefore had to be made whereby key posts were conceded to other parties to compensate for DC control of 'their' ministries. In this way, for example, the PSI and Social Democrats were allowed some control over the Ministry of Labour and Social Insurance (which controls pensions and unemployment benefits). These trade-offs contributed to the development of the spoils-sharing system, in which ministerial posts, positions on the administrative boards of public sector corporations and so on were shared out in rough proportion to the share of the vote gained by the parties. Even the PCI became included in this system when its electoral strength became a real threat to the collusive arrangements between the traditional governing parties. In a well known example, control over the public broadcasting corporation, the RAI, was shared out among the DC, PSI and PCI in 1975, on the eve of the PCI's inclusion in the government of national unity. The DC and PSI controlled the two best-resourced channels, RAI 1 and RAI 2, respectively. In exchange for not obstructing this deal, the PCI was given control over the less important RAI 3. Thus, as the system of spoils-sharing extended with the momentum of mutual benefit and the emulation of success, even the PCI, the main party of opposition, showed it could be a willing participant.

The electoral reform movement

From the beginning of the 1990s, even before the corruption scandals of 1992–3, public perceptions of governmental complacency and lack of accountability gave momentum to a campaign for electoral reform. The blame for Italy's problems was, in fact, laid mainly at the door of PR and the fragmented party system it was perceived as sustaining.

The campaign for electoral reform was set up in spring 1990 by a group of dissident Christian Democrats led by Mario Segni, a Catholic reformer with a long-standing revulsion for the DC system of power. The immediate objective of the campaign was to push through three referendums, intended to reform the preference vote and introduce simple majority systems in national and local elections. In the event, only the first of these referendums survived scrutiny by the Constitutional Court, the other two being declared inadmissible.

Popular support for electoral reform mounted, gradually transforming the campaign into a 'transverse party' uniting Segni's Catholic reformers with the ex-Communist Democratic Party of the Left (Partito Democratico di Sinistra, PDS), as well as a number of smaller parties. On the day of this first referendum, in June 1991, the reform movement polled a decisive victory: 62.5 per cent of the population voted and 95.6 per cent of these were in favour of reform. The turnout for the referendum was extraordinarily high in view of its mid-summer timing and the influence of the reform's opponents over the media. Although Bettino Craxi, the leader of the PSI, contemptuously invited the Italian people to 'go to the seaside' on the day of the vote, the electorate was not to be deflected. The reform the referendum enabled was actually relatively minor, but it was widely perceived as a start on the road to more radical changes that would permit the electorate a real choice in the selection of government.

The electorate's message to the political class was further reinforced at the general elections of April 1992, in which voters punished the traditional parties, of both government and opposition. The DC's share of the vote fell by 4.6 per cent from its 1987 level, taking it below the 30 per cent level for the first time in the history of the Republic. The PDS's share of the vote fell even more dramatically, from 26.6 per cent (as the

PCI) in 1987 to 16.1 per cent in 1992. Although much of this drop can be explained by the schism of Communist Refoundation, which polled nearly 6 per cent, it seemed that the voters' distaste for the particracy extended to the traditional opposition, too. The PSI, which had experienced a consistent upward trend in its support since Bettino Craxi had assumed the leadership in 1976, dropped from 14.3 per cent in 1987 to 13.6 per cent. The main benefactors of the flight from the old parties were the Lombard League (forerunner of the Northern League), which polled 23 per cent of the vote in Lombardy and nearly 9 per cent of the national vote. Others that did well included Communist Refoundation and the small left, ecologist and single-issue parties.

As the year progressed, the *Tangentopoli* or 'Bribesville' revelations transformed public unease with the political class into disgust and outrage. The movement for reform was now unstoppable. The necessary signatures were collected to launch a further series of referendums, the most important of which was for a drastic reduction in the PR element in elections to the Senate. Recognising the inevitability of the reformers' victory, the DC and its main coalition partners joined in the call for a yes vote – to do otherwise would be to identify themselves with the malpractice and corruption that the reform was intended to end. On 18 April 1993, 82.7 per cent of the voting electorate voted in favour of reform in a referendum whose turnout was 77 per cent.

In the face of this effective vote of no confidence by the electorate, the government resigned, to be replaced with a caretaker government headed by the ex-Governor of the Bank of Italy, Carlo Azeglio Ciampi. Under this government, in August 1993, the new predominantly first-past-the-post electoral rules were approved (see pp. 40–2).

The corruption scandals of 1992–3

Tangentopoli is the name commonly given to the series of corruption scandals first emerging from the northern city of

Milan, previously thought of as the model of modern and industrious virtue, in glowing contrast to the corruption-ridden bureaucracies of Rome. The exposures were set in train through the energetic and sustained work of a group of Milanese magistrates, a prominent member of which, Antonio Di Pietro, soon became something of a national hero.

From early 1992, the Mani Pulite (Clean Hands) team of magistrates began to expose the involvement of large numbers of Italian politicians and business persons in blatantly corrupt practices. Most commonly, these practices related to the offer of donations to party finances in exchange for public sector contracts. To put it plainly, contracts to carry out work for the State were routinely sold in return for kickbacks, which were divided up among colluding political parties. As the investigations proceeded, the confessions of those arrested implicated an ever-widening circle of the Italian political and business elite. The targets of the magistrates' investigations were, virtually by definition, well-to-do and hitherto respected business people, far from the stereotype of the hardened criminal. Most were quick to inform on their old associates, thus spreading the blame and laying the grounds for the justification that the system was to blame, rather than individuals. The first of the people Di Pietro's team had arrested, Mario Chiesa, set the scene for those to follow with the querulous justification that he 'was only doing his job'. The PSI politician Chiesa had been charged with extorting a £2,700 kickback on a cleaning contract for the nursing home he directed.

Once set in train, the scandals began to emerge almost daily. One year after Chiesa's arrest, there had been 130 arrests and twenty-five MPs had received official notification they were under investigation. By the time of the March 1994 general election, called to elect a new government under new electoral rules, fully 447 old-guard politicians, including five former Prime Ministers, had been investigated on various corruption-related charges. This was not just a few bad apples – a large part of the barrel itself was rotten, it seemed.

The tendency of governments to increase spending before an election is common, and in many countries besides Italy politicians attempt to bolster electoral support in regions or sectors by channelling extra resources to them. Nor is it unheard of for governments to respond to the needs of powerful interest groups, especially ones that make donations to party funds. Although such practices are unpalatable to the less cynical, they are not necessarily illegal. In Italy, however, the intensity of inter-party competition drove extraordinary numbers of politicians over the boundaries of legality in the search for party funds and this, combined with the unleashing of the judiciary's potential independence, made the corruption scandals exceptional among Western democracies.

Particracy and corruption

The equation of jobs with votes and even the allocation of governmental posts to the parties in accordance with electoral strength are not specific to Italy. However, it is probable that the rule by the parties, in which men and women not directly accountable to parliament and hence the people can exercise tremendous power on the sole basis of their control of a sizeable package of votes, was nowhere else so deeply entrenched. The mechanisms of this particracy were self-reinforcing. The more votes a politician could muster, the greater was his or her prestige and standing within the party. Greater prestige in the party in turn increased access to political spoils and the means of patronage, and thus votes. But standing within the party could also be increased by making strategic use of donations by clients to party funds. The securing of such donations enhanced the individual's prestige and could even be used to finance the lavish entertainment needed to build and consolidate the networks of contacts that were vital to political advancement. As party rivalry became increasingly fierce and as electoral campaigns became increasingly expensive, it is hardly surprising that the currency of the hidden exchanges was often money as well as votes. Thus the practices of patronage and clientelism merged seamlessly into downright corruption. The principle of exchange was the same, and many of the politicians and business people found to be involved in the exchange of party financing for patronage seemed only dimly aware, if at all, that their activities could be seen as scandalous.

The collapse of the traditional parties

The public laundering of the nation's dirty and tangled linen by Di Pietro and the Mani Pulite pool of magistrates had a deeply traumatic effect. In the general election of 1992, with the worst of the scandals still to emerge, the shock waves had trembled the post-war party system without toppling it. But by the time of the local elections in June and especially December 1993 the enormity of the scandal had registered: of a total of 221 mayors elected in *comuni* with more than 15,000 inhabitants, only nine were DC candidates. The death knell had tolled for the dominant party of the post-war coalitions and its junior partners, especially the PSI.

Explaining the crisis

The hidden exchanges that oiled the wheels of transactions between the State and citizens, the public and the private spheres, had permeated deep into the expectations of the Italian public. Even before the revelations of 1992 on, few Italians would have been astonished to learn that a certain official was prepared to speed up some paperwork through the bureaucracy in return for a *bustarella* – an envelope of money. Furthermore, seen in a general sense, the system actually worked quite well for most. Despite ups and downs, the Italian economy continued to flourish and the system of patronage functioned to provide for many of those citizens who were at the most severe disadvantage, just as did the more transparent welfare provisions set up elsewhere in Europe. Italian citizens, while manifesting a comparatively high degree of dissatisfaction with their political leadership, were relatively well off in European terms. Had the system remained veiled from the public gaze, however thinly, it is possible that it could have continued more or less indefinitely without serious challenge. But that was not to be. From the late 1980s, the conditions which had sustained particracy and made it possible for Italy to live with systemic corruption changed radically.

The explanation of the unmasking of corruption and the final collapse of the traditional parties of coalition involves a number of interrelated factors:

First, the main catalyst for the exposure of the particracy was the collapse of Communism in East Europe. The fall of the Berlin Wall in 1989 led many to claim the final triumph of capitalism over its historical foe. Some even went so far as to proclaim the 'end of history': the system of free and open markets favoured by the USA had proved its superiority and established itself as the final stage of history, the pinnacle of human achievement. In deference to the global certification of the death of Communism, in 1991 the PCI became the PDS. The main reason for the existence of the DC – its role as a bulwark against Communism and the real or imagined threat it posed to the free play of market forces – had been pulled away. Automatic collusion in the corrupt practices of the DC and its coalition partners could no longer be perceived as a requirement for the survival of liberal democracy in Italy.

Second, particularly in the wealthy north of Italy, the disadvantages of an inefficient and corrupt public sector were beginning to outweigh any advantages that citizens, and especially businesses, gained from patronage. As competition between the parties became increasingly intense and the expense of running electoral campaigns increased, the price extracted for the allocation of a public sector contract or other favours rose concomitantly. The motivation for businesses to collude to hide the corrupt exchanges was progressively weakened: the price of preferential treatment had become too high.

Third, it was increasingly evident that the price of clientelism and its corollary, corruption, could no longer be afforded by the Italian economy as a whole. Clientelism required a continual increase in public spending, as favoured client groups pressed for their relative advantages to be maintained and previously excluded groups demanded compensations, such as the improvements in wage earners' pension rights. The result was a rapid burgeoning of Italy's public debt. In 1970, this stood at 33.7 per cent of gross domestic product. In 1990 it had reached 52.3 per cent and by 1992 a startling 102.7 per cent. The debt burden was especially alarming to business as it became apparent, following the Maastricht Treaty, that Italy's membership of the European Union core could be threatened if public spending cannot be dramatically reduced.

Fourth, the political space for the expression of disaffection with the DC had been provided by the Lombard League, a populist regional movement whose invective against the drain on national resources – largely generated in the north – represented by the inefficient, corrupt and increasingly southernised State sector struck a chord with the northern middle class – especially given the burden on taxes posed by servicing Italy's crippling public deficit. The new party's share of the vote rose from 0.5 per cent in the general election of 1987 to 8.7 per cent in 1992 – an astonishing result for a regionally based party in a national election, especially in view of Italy's multi-party system.

Throughout the Cold War, fear of Communism was the characterising feature of the Italian polity. The rapid entrenchment of a multi-party system dominated by the DC was its most visible effect, giving rise in turn to practices of spoils-sharing and the ad hoc use of resources to essentially political ends.

Italy's lack of an eligible opposition thus lies at the heart of any explanation of the extraordinary events of the early

1990s. In recognition of this, the next chapter explores the absence in Italy of a unified left-of-centre party that could have provided an alternative government and perhaps prevented the emergence of particracy.

Further reading

Calise, M. 'The Italian Particracy: Beyond President and Parliament', *Political Science Quarterly*, Vol. 109 (1994).

Furlong, P. 'Political Catholicism and the Strange Death of the Christian Democrats', in Gundle, S. and Parker, S. (eds), *The New Italian Republic*, London (1996).

On patronage and public administration see Cassese, S. 'Hypotheses on the Italian Administrative System', *West European Politics*, Vol. 16, No. 3 (1993).

For a classic model of the Italian party system see Sartori, G. 'A Typology of Party Systems', reproduced in Mair, P. (ed.), *The West European Party System*, Oxford (1990).

5

The left

Introduction

In many European countries, the development of mass political parties representing working people was followed by their inclusion in some way in political power. The promise to 'responsible' parties of the left that they might be allowed to wield some influence within capitalism was a strong motivation to socialist parties to curb their more radical elements and develop moderate programmes of reform. However, this process of incorporation occurred only to a very limited extent in Italy. This is an important part of the explanation of why reformist leaderships have never achieved a thorough domination of the left in Italy.

Some attempts at conciliation with the working and peasant classes were made in the liberal era, notably under the premiership of the consummate politician Giolitti. But his strategy was thwarted by the strong conservative forces (representing especially the landowners and nobility, the monarchy, the military and the Church) that were deeply influential in parliament. Weakened by their inability to achieve reforms that could improve the lot of ordinary people, the reformists in the PSI were increasingly marginalised through the period of the liberal regime.

The Italian socialist movement was further radicalised by the impact of the First World War. Italy's intervention was deeply unpopular in the country and the misery and acute repression suffered by the many could be contrasted with the luxuries of those who had profited from the war. Elsewhere in Europe, the left had been at least partially brought behind the national war efforts and was temporarily reconciled with the ruling classes in the belief that the nation had to be defended against foreign aggression and authoritarianism. But no such broadly based national patriotism developed to heal Italy's divisions. The First World War was followed by an acute radicalisation of the peasant and worker movements, but also by their division, in part at least because the peasants who had in large part fought the war were resentful of the attitudes of the anti-interventionist industrial workers, many of whom had stayed in Italy to keep the factories working.

The foundation of the PCI

The Communist Party of Italy (forerunner of the PCI) origi-nated as a split-off from the PSI in January 1921 during the seventeenth congress of the PSI at Leghorn (Livorno). Its formation followed years of calls to expel the reformists from the PSI, and the increasing favour shown to the Communist faction by the leadership of the new Soviet Union. Its main nucleus was made up of an important anarcho-syndicalist faction under the leadership of Amadeo Bordiga and the New Order group that had formed in Turin around the activist and theoretician Antonio Gramsci.

In the earliest years of its formation, under Gramsci's influ-ence, the PCI recognised the need for a flexible approach that could appeal beyond the industrial working class that formed the core of its membership to, especially, the peasantry, who still made up the bulk of the population. Emblematic of this approach was the production of a daily paper, *L'Unità* (Unity), first published in early 1924. By late 1924, the PCI had 12,000 members and *L'Unità* had a readership of 20,000.

In 1922, Mussolini came to power on the wave of the right-wing backlash to the massive upheavals of the period immediately following the First World War. In November 1926, as Fascism's grip on society tightened, all parties in opposition to the regime were banned and forced to go underground. The leadership of the PCI was dispersed. Gramsci was arrested, and years of detainment worsened his ill-health. He died in 1937, shortly after being granted his freedom. Palmiro Togliatti, another Turin activist and Gramsci's successor as party leader, went into exile in Moscow. Other leaders were also exiled, either abroad or internally, confined to remote villages in the south and on islands.

But, clandestinely, the PCI as an organisation fared somewhat better than the PSI. In part, this was because of its better links to international socialism and especially to the Soviet Union. In part, too, it was simply more successful in sustaining networks, especially among the industrial working class. In fact, clandestine Communist cells continued to exist in most of the large factories of the north.

The Resistance

From 1943, resistance to Fascism emerged in the urban centres of the north, where strikes and industrial sabotage weakened the Fascist and Nazi war effort by curtailing access to the products of the big metalworking factories, where the means of warfare were produced. At the same time, groups of anti-Fascist fighters took to the hills to take on the enemy militarily.

Communists played a key role in the Resistance movement. Organised in the Garibaldi brigades, they made up more than 70 per cent of the partisans. Their organisational skills and capacity for discipline were crucial in the leadership of city insurrections, strikes, sabotage and guerrilla warfare. The task of the Allied forces, who had landed in the south in September 1943 and were fighting their way up the peninsula, was made much easier by the rapidly growing Resistance movement that, for the next eighteen months, waged its own war on Fascism.

Because of their role in the defeat of Fascism, the left, and particularly the Communists, were key elements in the committees of national liberation (*comitati di liberazione nazionale*, CLNs) that were the first organs of political power to emerge as Fascism retreated. The DC, which had formed in 1942, played a very minor role in these. However, the US and UK forces had no intention of allowing the Resistance movement and its committees to retain political authority. The Allies had resurrected the institutions of the old State in the conservative south before the north was liberated and they did not want to see its authority undermined by the existence of an alternative. Although the partisans were allowed to supervise their own disarming, the Resistance was effectively forced to surrender and its organs of political power were gradually dismantled. The PCI complied in this process willingly, pinning its hopes in sharing power in the future, when the immediate objective of national liberation had been fully achieved.

However, enormous prestige had accrued to the men and women of the left who had shown such heroism and efficiency in the overthrow of Fascism. Popular support for the PCI grew rapidly. By the time of the elections to the Constituent Assembly in 1946, it stood at 19 per cent of the electorate, against the nearly 21 per cent obtained by the PSI. The PCI was rather disappointed by this result, but it would not be long before the PCI would fulfil its ambition of overtaking the PSI and displacing it as the main party of the left.

The nature of Italian Communism

Already, on his return to Italy in March 1944, Togliatti had mapped out the strategy of the PCI. The immediate objective was to join with all other anti-Fascist forces in Italy to defeat Fascism. After that, the Communists would work within the new democracy for a major but gradual transformation of the socio-economic fabric of society. This he called progressive democracy. The PCI leader was especially clear on one point:

there was to be no insurrectionary seizure of power. The restoration of bourgeois democracy was not even to be seen as a transitional stage on the way to socialism and the abolition of capitalism. Although the term was ambiguous, Togliatti's progressive democracy, based on a high degree of political participation by the people, was a goal in itself.

The strategy by which this goal was to be achieved involved the establishment of a coalition of anti-Fascist forces, including the DC, whose supporters included many ordinary people of the working class. The leadership of the PCI was in fact convinced that the Catholic and Communist mass parties were bound by a common philosophy of fraternity and social solidarity. The strategy of reconciliation with the DC – a reconciliation that was to involve not just the social bases of the DC but also its leadership – was pursued with unwavering determination through the course of the post-war Republic, in the face of mounting evidence that the DC leadership had no intention whatsoever of sharing power with the PCI.

Of course, the post-war Communist commitment to progressive democracy and permanent alliance with the forces of Christian Democracy were not everywhere believed. Many Communists, including local leadership levels, preferred to see the new course laid out by Togliatti as a smoke screen, a device to buy time to prepare for the coming battle for the establishment of socialism. Even more crucially for the nature of post-war Italian democracy, most of the non-Communist political forces were deeply sceptical, maintaining that the PCI was a wolf in sheep's clothing, whose true nature would be revealed if it were allowed to assume office. The importance of this deeply rooted fear cannot be overestimated in an explanation of the politics of post-war Italy.

At the end of the war, as well as establishing the long-term strategy of the PCI, Togliatti had also determined to change its organisational base. The PCI would become a new party that would admit to its ranks even those with scant knowledge of Marxism, although its cadres would still receive proper training. The new party was a highly successful vehicle of recruitment. By 1946, the PCI had a membership of over two million. The DC had little option but to include the two parties of the left in the post-war tripartite governments.

The defeat and exclusion of the left

The anti-Fascist coalition including the left did not last long. In May 1947, the DC leader Alcide De Gasperi unceremoniously ousted the left from power and established a centre coalition with the lay parties. In June 1947, the hard man Mario Scelba was appointed Minister of the Interior, from which position he rapidly purged the police not of Fascists but of former partisans, and encouraged them to intervene ruthlessly at the first sign of peasant or working-class protest.

At same time, the economically liberal Luigi Einaudi, as Finance Minister, implemented a tight credit squeeze to curb inflation. In this project he was successful, but the social costs were high. Investment declined, many firms were forced to make redundancies and unemployment rose sharply.

The left had fallen far indeed from its high point of participation in political and industrial decision-making in the immediate post-war period. For the decade that followed the end of the tripartite experiment, the conditions of the Italian urban and rural working classes remained wretched in comparison with Italy's northern European neighbours, and the absence of a strong political voice for reform goes some way to explaining this. Where elsewhere welfare states were set up, democratic institutions were strengthened and workers enjoyed rising wages as the fruit of their rapidly increasing productivity, Italy had minimal social protections, some of the lowest wage rates in Europe and political closure as the DC steadfastly resisted the implementation of the politically inclusive and progressive elements of the constitution.

Given the initial strength of the left in the immediate post-war period, the capacity of the DC to expel it from government with such ease requires some further explanation. In fact, despite its prestige among a large section of the population, the left faced a number of serious problems in the immediate post-war period.

The weakness of the left

A number of factors contributed to the window of opportunity that allowed the DC in 1947 to exclude the left from government and assert its own domination of the political system. As in the rest of Europe, the bargaining power of the Italian working class was severely weakened by the economic conditions of the immediate post-war period, in which large-scale unemployment strengthened the employers' hand as workers could easily be replaced from the great pool of people seeking work. However, this general weakness was compounded in Italy by a number of other factors.

The Cold War and anti-Communism

First and foremost was the ideological momentum of anti-Communism, which was particularly strong in Italy. Italy, with its geographical location between West and East, and with its political status as the home of the largest Western Communist party, was a profound worry to the USA in its new role as world policeman. The major foreign-policy objective of the US political leadership of the time was to preserve the European liberal democracies and ensure that free markets in Europe would be safeguarded and open to US products. A priority in the pursuit of this objective was to prevent the PCI from gaining power or influence, and US interference in Italian affairs was quite open and unabashed. An account of US anti-Communist activities in the post-war period is given on pages 179–80.

The anti-Communist message was also hammered in by the Catholic Church. The theme of the family became central and the threat posed by Communism to the family and the values founded in it was driven home from pulpits all over the land.

The dense network of associations set up by the Church in the fields of education, recreation and charitable work had been allowed to thrive under Fascism and was quickly mobilised to the anti-Communist cause.

Internal divisions

Another problem of the left was the division of the labour movement, itself a product of Cold War tensions. In 1948, with the blessing of the Vatican, the Catholics split from the trade union confederation to form a separate Italian Confederation of Workers' Unions (Confederazione Italiana Sindacati Lavoratori, CISL). The Republicans and Social Democrats also split off shortly afterwards, forming the Italian Union of Labour (Unione Italiana del Lavoro, UIL). The Communists and Socialists remained in the largest of the three confederations, the Italian General Confederation of Labour (Confederazione Generale Italiana del Lavoro, CGIL). The different strands had previously been glued by the bond of their common anti-Fascism, but the break-up of the tripartite coalition inevitably led to their dissolution.

The split left the Communist-dominated CGIL in isolation. The other two confederations were favoured by management and, under pressure of the threat of loss of US business, often collaborated with management to depose the CGIL from its domination of the workplace. In a moment of high symbolism for the working class, the CGIL lost its majority on the organs of workers' representation in FIAT in the mid-1950s.

PCI strategy

A further weakness of the left can be identified in the strategy of the PCI itself. At least with a retrospective understanding of the nature and intentions of the DC leadership, the PCI's strategy of reconciliation with it appears disingenuous. Its pursuit of compromise with the DC often amounted to little more than submission. The agreement by the PCI representatives in the

Constituent Assembly, after minimal debate, to include the Concordat in the new constitution was symbolic of what was to come. Its inclusion effectively reversed Italy's pre-Fascist status as a secular State and gave constitutional authority to the strong influence of the Church on education. This major concession to the Church did not even achieve its immediate objective, which was the continued participation of the PCI in the governing coalition.

More serious in its implications for the organising capacity of the working class was, however, the decision to prioritise anti-Fascist national unity and the effort of national reconstruction to the effective exclusion of all other objectives. The Communist-dominated trade union confederation urged its members to show restraint in the pursuit of claims around their terms and conditions of employment, as wage pressure would hamper reconstruction and risk increasing unemployment. However, neither the PCI nor the unions developed a coherent alternative economic programme around which working people could be mobilised, so the insistence on restraint amounted to little more than an invitation to employers to drive wages down and productivity up. The messages of Togliatti and De Gasperi to the working classes were thus identical: the acceptance today of poor wages and a harsh regime of work would be rewarded later, when Italy had been lifted from its knees. The PCI's failure to give leadership to the workers in pursuit of their immediate interests had a pernicious effect on morale, especially as increasing unemployment and rising prices undermined the living standards of ordinary people in Italy.

The economic miracle

By the 1960s, however, a new era was dawning for Italy. From a poor and largely agrarian nation, Italy underwent a very rapid transformation to become one of the most important economies in Europe, together with Germany, France and the UK. The Christian Democratic State did not implement indicative economic planning on the French model, or actively foster a harmonious and consensual path in economic development, as in Germany, or construct a welfare system that would shelter workers 'from the cradle to the grave', as in the UK. But it had not been inactive at the level of the economy. For example, major infrastructural work had taken place, improving transport and communications, and a State holding company had reorganised steel production, ensuring a cheap and plentiful supply to industry of this fundamental material. Italy had also reversed its tradition of protectionism with its entry as a founding member of the European Coal and Steel Community and soon benefited from the increase in foreign trade.

And as we have seen, Italian employers enjoyed a particular advantage in export markets. The weakness of the trade unions gave them a virtual free hand in the factory. Productivity was pushed up remorselessly, from a base of 100 in 1953 to 162 in 1960, while real wages actually fell slightly. It was on these bases that the Italian economic miracle was built and Italy was catapulted into the modern world.

But entry into the world of modern, industrial Europe brought with it increasingly insistent voices for the sorts of economic and social reforms that would afford a measure of protection to working people and bring Italy in line with its European neighbours.

The opening to the left

By the beginning of the 1960s, the perennially divided DC was experiencing internal problems as the factions battled for the leadership of the party and the governing coalition became increasingly unstable. In 1960, following a government crisis, the President of the Republic asked the right-winger Fernando Tambroni to form a government, a task that he was able to fulfil only with the support of the neo-Fascist party, the MSI. The Tambroni government was a fiasco. When the MSI attempted to hold its national congress in Genoa, a city that had been a centre of the Resistance movement and where anti-Fascist sentiment ran high, an anti-Fascist demonstration ended in riots and running battles with the police. The response of the government was to authorise the police, in emergencies, to shoot demonstrators. Over the following days a number of anti-government protesters were shot dead during demonstrations and even more were seriously wounded. In protest at the deaths, the trade unions called a general strike, which received massive support. At last Tambroni was persuaded to stand down and order was restored. But the events of 1960 showed that a government supported by the successors to the Fascist Republic of Salò would not be tolerated. The governing coalition would have to be opened to the left, not the right.

The conditions for such a shift had in fact matured. The Cold War was thawing somewhat under Kennedy's presidency of the USA and even the Church was now tempering its anti-Communist crusade with a new emphasis on social justice. What is more, there were growing fears – at home and abroad – that a continued refusal to include the PSI in government could drive it towards the Communists. In December 1963, after a period of support for the governing coalition, the PSI at last became part of government.

The government of the centre-left raised very high expectations – a dangerous thing to do in politics if they are not then met. And in Italy, they were not. Throughout the 1960s, hopes were continually raised, only to be dashed. The promise to establish the regional assemblies foreseen by the constitution came to nothing. Other planned reforms, of agricultural contracts, of town planning, of the educational system, were either shelved or so watered down as to have little impact. The electricity industry was nationalised, but in a way that left its management very little changed.

The problems of the PSI

The PSI's participation in government did not do it any good in political or electoral terms. The left of the party split off in

1964 to form the Socialist Party of Proletarian Unity. In 1966 the rightward move of the PSI facilitated a merger with the Social Democrats, who had split from the PSI in 1947 with the encouragement of the USA. However, the merger did not fulfil the PSI's hopes that it could become an electorally attractive force distinct from both DC and PCI, and the two parties split again after a few years. The PSI's lack of a clear identity of its own had long been a problem, contributing to its failure to become the major party of the left. Now this problem was compounded by its lacklustre performance in the centre-left governments. It had secured only very minimal reform and did not appear to have any clear programme other than keeping the centre-left coalition alive and thus ensuring its own continued participation in power.

The return to militancy

In the meantime, the populations of the great industrial cities of the north were growing at unprecedented rates, as immigrants flooded in from the rural areas, and especially from the south, to work in the factories that were churning out the new mass-produced goods of the consumer age. The rapid growth of the industrial centres placed huge pressures on services and infrastructures. The provision of housing, health care, transport and education was totally inadequate to meet the needs of the burgeoning populations. Conditions inside the factories, too, were extremely harsh. Workers received very little legal protection with regard to standards of health and safety in the factories, and wages, as we have seen, were very low by standards elsewhere in Europe.

What is more, the demand for labour was now outstripping its supply in some sectors, strengthening the workers' hand in relation to the employers. In conjunction with the expectations raised by the long-awaited inclusion of the left in government, the scene was set for a new mood of worker militancy. In the context of the harsh attitudes of the employers and the State's failure to mitigate conditions of life and employment, this mood was almost bound to be explosive.

The first signs of the new militancy came from the early 1960s. Strikes and demonstrations occurred in a variety of places. The most famous of these culminated in the riots of Piazza Statuto in Turin in 1962, in which young FIAT workers engaged in a two-and-a-half-day running battle with the police, despite calls to disperse from the national trade union leaderships. Throughout the 1960s, days lost to strike actions continued to rise and the workers gained important concessions on wages. In other countries, governments and industrialists were often able to rely on trade union leaderships to moderate workers' demands in return for improvements in wage rates or consultation over managerial decisions. But in Italy this option had been lost. The trade union movement had been profoundly weakened and divided in the late 1940s and early 1950s. Without firmly rooted institutions in the work-place or a united confederation, the trade unions could do very little to influence the course of events.

The youth and worker movements of the late 1960s

The industrial working class was not the only sector of the population to assert itself against the establishment in the 1960s. The expansion of higher education in the 1960s in Italy, as elsewhere in Europe, had contributed to the emerg-ence of a strong student and youth movement. In Italy, as in France, the mood of protest was further fuelled by the inad-equacy of educational reforms, which had expanded student numbers while doing little to improve facilities, or reform authoritarian institutional structures and outdated courses. But unlike in France, the youth and student movement in Italy was able to form a strong and relatively lasting bond with the workers' movement. Extra-parliamentary groupings such as Lotta Continua ('the struggle goes on') were per-meated by a new sort of left thinking in which the centralism and bureaucracy of the traditional parties of the left were rejected in favour of a more open and participatory style, and there was a generalised impatience with a parliamentary route to reform that in Italy had born so few fruits.

In Turin, a semi-permanent worker–student assembly sprang up on the premises of the university teaching hospital, meeting nearly every day from May to July 1969 to discuss demands and strategy, develop slogans and produce leaflets and bulletins. The workers began to elect a new sort of representative, the *delegato* (delegate, or shop steward), who had no necessary connection with the official trade unions and was instantly revocable by workmates. As the situation slipped out of trade union control, and *de facto* workers' leaders appeared and disappeared, management had difficulty in finding someone with the authority to negotiate on behalf of the workers. Union-called strikes were frequently extended and transformed into violent confrontations in which large groups of workers would march round the factories brandishing iron bars and banging on empty oil cans, sometimes even kidnapping managers. Sometimes the workers' struggles spilled out of the factories on to the streets, as in the battle of Corso Traiano on 3 July 1969, when a one-day strike for housing reform called by the trade union confederations spilled over into riots so furious that prisoner exchanges between police and demonstrators were alleged to have taken place.

Trade union renewal

The struggles of 1969 had profound effects on the nature of trade unionism in Italy and on the balance of power between employers and workers. The *delegati* were given official recognition by management and were largely incorporated within official trade union structures, improving communications between rank-and-file members and union leaderships. Trade union demands became more closely attuned to the interests of the semi-skilled workers, who predominated on the shop floor. The new demands were taken up by all of the three main trade union confederations and gave fresh impetus to the tendency towards unitary action, especially between the CGIL and CISL. The Communist and Catholic confederations began to loosen ties with 'their' parties, as policy divergences between the PCI and the DC may otherwise have threatened the still fragile cooperation within the trade union movement.

The workers' movement of the late 1960s secured important results. Wage rates rose rapidly, destroying Italy's status as a low-wage area. Wages were firmly linked to inflation, further undermining Italy's reliance on the export of low-priced consumer goods as a motor of economic growth. Perhaps most importantly of all, a Workers' Statute was passed into law, enshrining basic trade union rights and the right to appeal against unfair dismissal. Thus, at last, a legally binding framework of rights was in place, giving some concrete reality to the affirmation of the constitution that Italy was a 'Republic based on labour'.

The historic compromise

The general mood of increased working-class confidence from the 1960s had beneficial effects for the PCI, whose share of the national vote rose steadily through the 1960s and 1970s and surged to a historic peak of 34.4 per cent in the 1976 elections to the Chamber of Deputies.

However, the PCI did not use its new strength to launch a political attack on the DC, or to capitalise on the appeal of feminism and civil rights movements by emphasising the distinctiveness of its secular tradition in its approach, for example, to the family and education. Rather, under the new leadership of Enrico Berlinguer, it redoubled its efforts to forge a bond with the DC through the strategy of the historic compromise, launched in 1973.

The 1973 overthrow of the elected left-wing government in Chile was an important factor in the PCI's decision to pursue the historic compromise with the DC. For Berlinguer, the Chilean coup demonstrated the danger posed to Italian democracy by the conservative forces that still permeated the establishment. There is some justification for Communist anxieties that a determined effort to dislodge the DC from its dominant position in Italian politics might have resulted in an authoritarian coup. There is, in fact, evidence of the existence of conspiratorial networks linking the far right to elements within the military and secret services and even the political establishment in the 1970s. This evidence is treated in chapter 7.

With the strategy of the historic compromise the PCI wanted to usher in a new era of social and political inclusion in which it would use participation in government – which now seemed within its grasp for the first time since its ejection from the tripartite coalition in 1947 – to bring about major reforms of Italy's economic and social structures. The first priority, then, was to achieve a place in government. To do this, the leadership believed, the PCI would have to demonstrate that it was willing and able to restore order, restraint and predictability within the workers' and students' movements. Once the basis for stable economic and democratic growth had been restored, the DC would be unable to justify the continued exclusion of the PCI.

The PCI put pressure on the Communist-dominated CGIL to lead an about turn in the trade union movement. Under the new course, finally adopted in February 1978, the trade unions accepted economic growth as a priority. Wage rises were to be responsible and restrained, the terms of public assistance for the unemployed were to be reduced, mobility between sectors would be allowed to help solve problems of overstaffing (opening the way to mass redundancies, for example at FIAT in 1980), the demand for a shorter working week was renounced and a ceiling was to be placed on the public deficit. Already by 1977, the *Economist* (6 August) was able to note that 'the improvement in Italy's economy owes much to the restraining hand of the communists on Italy's unions'.

The PCI also developed an increasingly hard line towards the radical protest movements of the 1970s, adopting a language of law and order. Its lack of sympathy with the youth and protest movements of the 1970s was probably an important factor in the continuing growth of red terrorism in that period: the existence of a parliamentary party prepared to forward demands for the extension of political participation and the protection of civil liberties would have done much to isolate the practitioners of violence.

The governments of national unity

The DC, for its part, needed to offer an olive branch to the PCI. The impact of the oil crisis of 1973 was particularly severe in Italy, as the shortage of domestic energy resources meant industry relied heavily on oil imports and the price of these was now spiralling. The country's economic problems were compounded by a flight of capital triggered by the industrial unrest of the hot autumn. The collaboration of the working class to restore Italy's economic health had rarely been so essential.

Politically, too, the DC was under fire. The party was shocked by the results of the 1974 referendum in which the people refused to repeal the 1970 law permitting divorce. The referendum results showed the permeation of a new mood of rebellion even among the DC's core of support in the Catholic faithful, especially women. The DC was also worried by election results in the 1970s (see figure 4.1, p. 64). Its own vote remained stable: for many it was a source of safety in a climate of acute social tension. However, the PCI was making worrying advances at the expense of the smaller parties in the national elections of 1972 and 1976 and did very well in the regional elections of 1970 and especially 1975.

In August 1976, the PCI was asked to support a government of national unity. It was agreed that the PCI would abstain from voting against the government, in what has been called the 'not no-confidence' vote. In a second government of national unity, from January 1978, the PCI gave its active support to the coalition. In return, the PCI was offered no ministerial posts, although it was given the presidency of the Chamber of Deputies and about one-quarter of the chairs of the powerful parliamentary committees. It is unlikely that the DC ever saw collaboration with the PCI as anything more than a temporary expedient that could be abandoned once order was restored.

The legacy of the governments of national unity

Throughout the short history of the governments of national unity, the PCI played a subordinate role. It made little headway with plans for increasing investment and employment, especially in the south, that had been the centrepiece of its programme.

The record of the 1976–9 governments was by no means entirely negative. A number of important and long overdue reforms passed into law, notably the consolidation of Italy's disparate health provision into a National Health Service. However, as we shall see in the next chapter, the implementation of these reforms was profoundly flawed.

All in all, little had been gained from the PCI's participation in government by way of concrete reform. At the same time, the party's policy of sacrifice for the working class, and its tough stance towards youth and civil rights protest, had lost it much support among these natural constituencies of the left, and its participation in the spoils-sharing system had irrevocably tarnished its image as the clean party that had remained outside of the machinations of the particracy.

In 1979, the PCI returned to opposition and in the general elections held that summer its vote dropped by four percentage points to 30.4 per cent; its vote among young people dropped by as much as 10 per cent. The PCI's electoral support continued to languish through the 1980s.

The PSI's comeback

In the meantime, the PSI, under the leadership of Bettino Craxi, made something of a political comeback. A major theme of the party, in its efforts to distinguish itself from the PCI, became the need for institutional reforms that would increase the stability and effectiveness of government. The most important of the reforms advocated by Craxi was a change to a presidential form of government in the French style, in which power would be concentrated in a powerful directly elected President.

Under Craxi's leadership, the party showed its ability to compete and win in the spoils-sharing system. By the early 1980s, the PSI had been able to secure a number of cabinet positions and a much larger share of key non-governmental posts than ever before in the history of its rather stable alliance with the DC. Following the sharp decline of the DC's share of the votes in the 1983 elections (from 38.3 to 32.9 per cent), Craxi was even able to secure the premiership. Craxi was Prime Minister from 1983 to 1987, an unusually long duration in Italian politics. However, the party under his leadership lost any remaining ideological identity as a party of the left. Craxi's stand for *decisionismo* – government based on effective, personalised leadership rather than the fudge of compromise – did not lead to great electoral successes and the party's increasing embroilment in the politics of particracy eventually led to its own and its leader's disgrace and political demise.

Further reading

Amyot, G. *The Italian Communist Party*, London (1981).
Cammett, J. M. *Antonio Gramsci and the Origins of Italian Communism*, Stanford (1967).
Ginsborg, P. *A History of Contemporary Italy: Society and Politics 1943–1988*, London (1990).
Hellman, S. *Italian Communism in Transition: The Rise and Fall of the Historic Compromise in Turin, 1975–1980*, Oxford (1988).

Hellman, S. 'The Left and the Decomposition of the Party System in Italy', in Miliband, R. and Panitch, L. (eds), *Socialist Register*, London (1993).

6

State, citizens and welfare

Welfare states in Europe

After the Second World War, the industrial nations of the
Western world all saw a continued growth of State activity
and a multiplication of the forums in which citizen and State
met. In the West European countries, the long post-war economic boom was accompanied by the development of strong
national welfare systems, in which employees were offered
considerable protection against the major risks that they ran:
unemployment, sickness and the inability to continue to work
and secure wages in old age. Part of the profits from rising
productivity, especially in the factories making the mass-
produced goods of the new consumer society, was returned to
employees, through general taxation or through employer/
employee contributions, providing the funding for payments to
those who were unemployed, sick, disabled and elderly. Another part of the benefits gained from increasing technical and
organisational efficiency went to fund health and social services, which especially helped the poor and infirm, as they
provided a sort of benefit in kind, as services the individual
would otherwise have had to pay for were provided free or at
low cost.

The European welfare states, and the simultaneous expansion of secondary and higher education to cover larger and
larger proportions of the population, gave many benefits to
employers, as well. The general health of the population from

which they drew their labour forces was improved, standards of literacy rose and a 'new' middle class, qualified to work in the white-collar jobs in the rapidly growing service sector, was created. Social welfare and education systems also did much to improve the lot and the opportunities of working people, fostering a sense of citizenship and inclusion within society and laying the basis for improved relations between workers and employers.

The modern industrialised nations had learned the dreadful lessons of the great depression of the 1930s and two world wars. To varying extents, protections against poverty and starvation were introduced and national health and education systems were set up to guard against the evils of want, disease and ignorance.

The post-war period also saw the extension of political participation and civil rights, as increasingly educated populations pressed for a voice in the institutions that framed their lives. Many countries have seen a devolution of decision-making out from central government towards more local levels, thus increasing citizens' access to the political system and giving them a more powerful voice in decisions that affect them. In some countries, such as Germany, the post-war period also saw a gradual extension of the rights of employees to be consulted about decisions that would affect the terms and conditions of their employment.

As women were drawn into the expanding labour force, provisions were made to enable them to combine work and family responsibilities, for example through the provision of nurseries and after-school care. Increasingly, women demanded and got some protection of their rights at work, in the shape especially of equal opportunity legislation. In the family, women gained more control over the course of their own lives through reforms of laws regulating such aspects as inheritance, divorce, access to contraception and information on birth control, and in some cases abortion.

The development of universal guarantees and legal protections did not, of course, proceed in a uniform way across all the countries of West Europe. In Italy, however, the process of recasting the pact between State and citizen appears particularly slow and piecemeal.

Redistribution of wealth and the prevention of poverty

Pensions

As in some other European mainland countries, pensions in Italy have been one of the main instruments for shifting wealth, whether this is from the rich to the poor (or vice versa), from one geographical region to another, or from one period in an individual's life cycle to another. Pensions have been, and still are, a very important instrument of redistribution in Italy, virtually substituting for transfer payments such as the unemployment benefits that are common in countries such as the UK. Because of this they will be treated at some length here.

There are four types of public occupational pension schemes in Italy. The main one covers blue- and white-collar private sector employees, while others cover the self-employed, public employees, and other special categories. Most of these schemes are administered by the National Institute for Social Insurance (Istituto Nazionale di Previdenza Sociale, INPS), which pays over 90 per cent of all pensions and has over seventeen million members. The INPS is governed by representatives drawn from the trade unions, employers and self-employed and by the Ministry of Labour. The scheme for private sector employees is financed by contributions from earnings, the employer paying two-thirds and the employee one-third. The comparatively high proportion of these contributions paid by the employer may encourage businesses to employ people illegally or, in the case of larger private industries, to reduce their payrolls, for example by contracting work out. The social insurance system thus contributes to the distinctive patterning of the Italian political economy with its very large sectors of self-employed and small businesses and high numbers of people in the submerged economy of irregular and informal forms of employment. The State covers any shortfall between the available funds and demands on them with special top-ups, a practice which is particularly common in the case of the scheme for the self-employed.

Until 1969, no State pension was available for old people with low incomes who had not been paying into a scheme. In the 1950s, coverage by social insurance was among the lowest in Europe, leaving people extremely vulnerable to the common risks of life such as loss of work, injury, illness and infirmity. It was only by the early 1970s that Italy was catching up with European average levels of protection.

The redistribution of wealth: north to south

An interesting and peculiarly Italian use of disability pensions appeared from around the time that emigration began to slow and the remittances sent back to the family members who had remained behind began to dry up. The rules of eligibility were changed to remove the need for a medically certified disability and to make living in an economically disadvantaged area a sufficient condition for receipt of the pension. This rule change was, of course, particularly beneficial to the poorer regions of the south, where the disability pension effectively became a form of unemployment benefit.

The pension system in Italy has quite strongly redistributory effects, but its main impact is geographical rather than social. In the north, every 100 lire of contributions give rise to payments in the form of pensions ranging from 83 in wealthy Piedmont to 150 in less wealthy Liguria. This effect is even stronger across the north–south dimension. Every 100 lire of contributions in the south give rise to an average payment of 250 lire.

Family access to pensions in the south (together with the money, or remittances, often sent back home by people who have emigrated) are obviously critical in underpinning the standard of living. However, they do not break the vicious cycle in which men of working age tend to emigrate to find work, leaving behind disproportionate numbers of the elderly, infirm and those with child-care responsibilities, who stand in most need of benefits. And while investment efforts have been made to create jobs in the south, all too often they have been guided by the need to bolster electoral support, rather than geared to the real economic potentialities of the region.

The redistribution of wealth: poor to rich

In terms of redistribution among wealthier and poorer groups in society in general, the effect is reversed: higher-income groups benefit more from their contributions than do the less well paid. This is in part because pensions are usually calculated on the basis of the last period of work before retirement, thus benefiting middle-class people who have pursued a career in which salaries increase with seniority and promotion. In part, it is also because the self-employed, often with the help of a canny accountant, can hide their real wealth, reducing the tax and contributions they pay. The approximately twelve million employees whose contributions are deducted from their salaries or wages have no such option. The self-employed are a very numerous group in Italy, including genuinely poor farmers alongside professionals and business persons.

The State colluded in the light tax burden shouldered by the self-employed and owners of small businesses, who were typically DC voters. Tax inspection is often lax or corrupt and many loopholes are left for legal tax avoidance. In 1985, under strong pressure from the trade unions, an attempt was made to tighten the procedures for VAT collection. A new law made it obligatory to hand over a proper receipt for purchases, making it difficult for shopkeepers, for example, to hide the extent of their sales. However, a very noticeable skew to the benefit of this sector remained. In the late 1980s it was estimated that 60–70 per cent of tax income derived from employees, despite the prevalence of self-employment and small businesses in the Italian economy.

In Italy, the unemployment benefit system is very un-developed and only very low rates are payable as of right. Those in temporary unemployment can receive payments from the Earnings Integration Fund (*Cassa Integrazione*), which is financed by contributions from the State and employer. Although there is a system of social assistance for those not eligible for employment-based benefits, it is not designed to provide a minimum guaranteed income to anyone with no other source of income (as is the case with the Job Seekers' Allowance in the UK). The social assistance system is operated by local government, along with social services and health care, and its terms and conditions vary across the country. This provides another opportunity for a geographical re-distribution of wealth, but leaves the long-term unemployed, especially in the north of Italy, without any form of safety net.

Pension reform

During the late 1960s, the three trade union confederations, backed by pensioners' demonstrations and strikes, were able to negotiate pension reform directly with government. This was the first time that Italy had experimented with the negotiation of socio-economic reform between trade unions and govern-ment. The trade union movement had moved beyond the negotiation of contracts between employee and employer to become an agent of political change. This experiment with neo-corporatism was seen to be reinforced with the appoint-ment of a trade unionist as president of INPS's administrative board. As a result of these and later reforms, employees in Italy – especially in the public sector and the strongly union-ised sectors – have extremely generous pensions. By the early 1990s, on the eve of the recent reforms, Italians were enjoy-ing some of the most generous pensions anywhere. The age for retirement was low, at sixty for men and fifty-five for women. Public employees were able to take early retirement after only twenty years of service, allowing many to enjoy a relatively leisured lifestyle before even reaching their forties. Pension levels were high and were maintained in real terms by indexation to the cost of living.

It is not surprising, then, that many working people in Italy see pensions as a major acquisition, a benefit to be defended at all costs. However, pensions account for up to 50 per cent of social expenditure, and as State spending rose to head-spinning levels, governments came under increasing pressure to cut them. This pressure is further increased by the plans for European Economic and Monetary Union (EMU). Italian participation in EMU depends on a radical pruning of State spending and public debt.

Attempts to cut back on the pensions bill have been met with very strong resistance. In October 1994, a four-hour general strike engaged ten million workers in protest against planned cuts in State pensions and in Rome, the following month, one and a half million Italians came together in the biggest demonstrations since 1945. The tide of public resentment enabled the trade union confederations to force a deal with government to mitigate the cuts. In 1995, under the government of Lamberto Dini, a reform that tended to reduce the generosity of pensions was negotiated with the unions, but the new system is being phased in gradually and is in any case unlikely to reduce overall pension expenditure in the long run. In early 1997, the centre-left Prodi government appointed a commission of experts to draft new welfare reforms. The commission's plans involve a significant rebalancing of a system which, as we have seen, favours particular sectors of the population and it is by no means certain that it will be acceptable to these sectors.

Given Italy's commitment to be an early participant in EMU, the issue of pensions is likely to continue to be a thorn in the side of Italian government for some time to come. Working people who have little other guaranteed source of income when they leave work plan the pattern of their lives in the expectation of a pension, and if the State reneges on promises made to them earlier in their working lives, there will inevitably be resentment.

Health

In the immediate post-war period, three major public institutions, inherited from Fascism, were directly responsible for health care. These were the INPS, the National Health Insurance Institution and the National Institute for Workers' Compensation. These public institutions appointed local general practitioners. They also administered some hospitals, although many treatments and services were contracted out to a multitude of hospitals and institutions, mainly run by the religious orders and operating in the uncertain area between the private and public sectors, known in Italy as the *parastato*.

The disparate provision led to enormous waste and inefficiency. The tasks of the institutions overlapped and were duplicated and there was no effective way of monitoring how the large sums of public money being spent on the system were used. The results for the users were interminable queues and waiting lists, frustrating bureaucratic procedures and, especially in the south, where the provision of hospital beds was low, overcrowded wards. The problems did not result in particular from underfunding – in these terms Italy compared fairly well with its northern European neighbours. Rather, the system was intractable to reform because it was inextricably linked into systems of patronage and clientelism.

In 1978, under the governments of national unity, which included the PCI, the chaotic and disparate provision of health care was unified into a single national health system through a consolidation of the insurance funds and hospital schemes. Control of the system was handed over to units supervised by elected local authorities. However, the new system did not lead to a break with the system of clientelistic use of public resources. The National Health Service was immediately colonised by the parties, as managers tended to be nominated on the basis of party strength in the municipal authorities. These political nominees could use their powers to create jobs and allocate contracts for the purposes of patronage. This, combined with the tendency of the public everywhere to use ever-increasing quantities of pharmaceuticals, medical tests and examinations and other services, led to spiralling costs.

Central governments since the 1980s have been concerned to gain a stronger control and audit of the system. The Ministry of Health now sets a budget for each region. The government can also fix the price of drugs and determine the number of people employed or contracted in the health sector and their level of pay.

Social services

Social services should also be included among the instruments that the State can use to ensure a decent standard of life to all citizens, including the poorest. The provision of both in Italy has always been, and remains, very thin. In the Italian welfare system, benefits in money, especially pensions, predominate over benefits in kind, such as free or cheap health care, housing, pre- and after-school child care, provisions such as home help for the elderly or infirm and help from social workers in the case of problems in the family.

Traditionally, social services were largely provided by the hundreds of private charitable and religious bodies. These have often received public funding to deliver services. The Catholic networks that provided the great bulk of social provision received cash injections from Marshall Aid, as well as State funding, in the early post-war period. State funding was given preferentially to the organisations of the Church, whose networks could thus be engaged in the defence of family values against the perceived threat of Communism. The Church's welfare arm organised educational and recreational activities, offering nurseries and after-school activities for children as well as seaside and mountain holiday camps. Many hospitals, nursing homes and institutions for the elderly were also run by the religious orders.

The provision of social services, like health provision, was thus fragmented and uncoordinated and there was no overall monitoring of the quality and relevance of the services offered. Provision frequently overlapped, many who worked within the system were incompetent or even indifferent, and anachronistic services often remained in place, as in the case of the national institute for war orphans which was still in receipt of large amounts of public money in 1975, thirty years after the end of hostilities.

Housing

The inadequate provision of public housing has also been a perennial problem in Italy, at its most acute at the height of emigration from the south to the north in the 1960s. Often recently arrived immigrants in cities like Turin had to sleep wherever they could, even in derelict buildings and cellars. Many shared rooms or even beds – it was not infrequent for a day-shift worker to vacate a bed for use by someone on the night shift. The housing shortage led to spiralling rents, putting what adequate housing there was out of the reach of the ordinary worker. Although this acute shortage had been resolved by the late 1960s, following the building (by private construction companies) of high-rise blocks on the peripheries of the cities, housing provision remained inadequate.

Some reform was achieved following the consolidation of trade union power from the late 1960s. In July 1969, the trade unions supported a strike against high rents and for the development of housing. In November, the action was extended with a general strike on the housing issue. The strike was massively supported and the government entered into direct negotiations with the trade unions on the issue of housing reform. The resulting law, which was finally enacted in 1971, had mixed results. Public money was allocated to fund a housing programme. Administration of public housing was handed over to local authorities, which were also given powers to expropriate building land with modest compensation to the previous owners. However, the usual problems of clientelism and more or less clear-cut corruption meant that only a small proportion of the money made available to build new public housing was appropriately spent.

In 1978, a rent-control law provided increased security of tenure to tenants and subjected rents to tests of fairness. The administration of the law was once again devolved to the local level. But as has happened so often in Italy, a law that on paper seemed to promise considerable protection for tenants proved flawed in practice. The increased security of tenants and the limitation on the rents that could be asked meant that many houses were simply kept empty as in any case inflation was increasing the value of the property. In many cases, the provisions simply made it more difficult to find decent accommodation at affordable prices.

The nature of welfare: a summary

The welfare system in Italy may be described by three key terms:

1 *Particularist*. Particular sections of the population tend to be targeted for help and benefits. Because most pensions are linked to occupation, particular occupational groups can be offered advantages from which others are excluded. Particular regions can also be targeted, as we saw in the case of disability benefit. This allowed successive governments to favour the poor in the south, a DC electoral heartland, while spending less in areas where the Communist vote tended to be high, such as industrialised urban areas.

2 *Incremental*. There has been virtually no long-term or even mid-term planning. Policy has largely involved the addition

of new bits of legislation, to set up and fund new agencies, according to expediency. This expediency has often been purely electoral, to bolster support especially among groups who might be expected to vote for the DC. However, increasingly since the 1969 watershed, policy change has responded to acute pressures from the trade unions or other social movements. Cabinet instability and the frequent reshuffles of ministerial teams is also a major factor in the incapacity to develop and implement coherent long-term plans for the welfare system.

3 *Non-progressive.* There has been little attempt to use welfare provision and benefits to redistribute wealth from the rich to the poor by using progressive taxation to fund services that would otherwise have to be bought. As a result, there has been very little change in the distribution of post-tax household incomes since the war and poverty remains an intractable problem, especially in the south.

The nature of welfare: explanations

It might be expected that the late and uneven development of welfare provision in Italy could be linked mainly to the exclusion of the left from effective governmental power throughout most of the post-war period. However, the development of more systematic provisions, especially in Italy's northern neighbours, was not exclusively an achievement of the left. While the UK's National Health Service was established by the post-war Labour government, it was defended and protected by successive Conservative governments and more recently has come under attack from both right and left. In Germany, one of the most generous and efficient systems of welfare benefits was perfected by the post-war coalition dominated by the centre-right, and this system continued as the centrepiece of the consensual relations and relatively egalitarian growth that characterised the German economy. Thus the predominance of centre-right governments in other countries did not prevent the establishment and continued funding of national welfare systems, or the extension of legal rights to ever-widening circles of the national community. Nevertheless, the conditions and mechanisms of DC domination of the political system are a fruitful place to begin a discussion of the particular form taken by the welfare system in Italy.

Although successive governments clearly recognised the shortcomings of the system – a variety of government enquiries have reported on diverse aspects of the welfare system – no radical reform was forthcoming until the late 1960s and the explosion of social movements of that time. Even thereafter, the concrete results of reforms have been very patchy. The central reason why reform was left so late and implemented so ambiguously is that the welfare system, as it stood, was an excellent tool for clientelistic use by the colluding parties. The fragmented agencies and non-universal benefits of the welfare system in Italy had a political, as well as social, function. Benefits (like the disability pension) could be targeted on those who were likely to vote for the status quo, while those who were not could be left to shoulder a disproportionate burden of taxes and contributions. The myriad agencies and quangos could be staffed by political allies and the State resources they administered used to favour supporters in the population and thus enhance the chance of re-election to power. Such a sensitive instrument of clientelism and patronage would not be given up without a struggle by those who most benefited from it, who were, of course, those who controlled it and were best placed to perpetuate it.

Participatory democracy: people's power in the community

So far this chapter has treated State–citizen relations in passive terms, looking at the State's role in providing basic resources and services to its people. But another important aspect of a State's relationship with its citizenry is the extent to which ordinary people can have an active voice in decision-making in the community and workplace.

Italians are frequently called to the polls, to elect representatives to the European parliament, municipal, provincial and regional governments, the Chamber of Deputies and the Senate. Turnouts are generally comparatively high, in elections at supranational and subnational as well as national level. The franchise, in line with other Western nations, is wide: women in Italy gained the right to vote only in 1946, but this can be explained by the intervention of two decades of Fascist rule. The age of majority was brought down from twenty-one to eighteen in 1975. But participation in a society's decision-making processes is not limited to the opportunity to vote in general elections, important as this is.

Local politics

Until the 1970s, the Italian political system was centralised and ultimate power largely resided in Rome. State-appointed prefects could overrule the decisions of elected local authorities, meaning that this level of citizen access to the decision-making process was very limited. The 1970 reform set up the regional assemblies and gave them some real powers to intervene in the local economy and social environment. However, this devolution of power was limited (see chapter 3). In this respect, however, Italy is not necessarily very anomalous. Whereas Germany, of course, has a strongly federal system, in which state (*Länder*) governments have wide powers and representation in the upper house, France was also a highly centralised State, in which a formal devolution of powers was not experimented with until the 1980s. The UK, on the other hand, recently experienced a period of prolonged recentralisation as Conservative administrations under Margaret Thatcher introduced increasing constraints on the spending powers and spheres of action of local governments.

In some localities, Italian citizens have had some real experience with participatory politics. In 1976, parliament passed a law making provisions for a potentially radical extension of the powers and functions of neighbourhood government. City governments could now decide whether or not to open neighbourhood councils to direct election instead of appointing the members. The neighbourhood councils could be given powers to appoint committees to oversee local provision of services, such as housing, health, public transport and day-care centres. Where local authorities decided to make full use of the law, as in Florence, an exciting experiment in popular participation ensued. However, uptake of the opportunity was limited. Even some left-dominated local authorities, such as that in Turin, deemed the experiment too risky and decided to appoint the neighbourhood councils in proportion to the relative electoral strengths of the parties.

Overall, the experimentation with devolution of power in Italy has been patchy. In too many cases, local government has been absorbed into the system of particracy, in which resources are seen as the property of the parties and are allocated and controlled according to party strengths.

Industrial democracy: the power of employees and trade unions

From the late 1960s, working people in Italy have enjoyed a rather remarkable extension of rights and protections at work, giving them a real voice in the decisions that in many other countries are considered the province of management alone. Although these rights were somewhat curtailed in the 1980s, trade unions still have a powerful industrial and political voice and employees retain a legacy of defences against managements whose only concern is profits.

Participation by employees in decision-making processes affecting their jobs and workplaces was extremely limited until the late 1960s. Large, private sector workplaces were characterised by authoritarian management philosophies, in which consultation of the workforce was seen as an unacceptable infringement of managerial prerogative. Major decisions, such as the introduction of new technologies and working methods, or mergers and relocations, could be taken with no reference to the employees or their representatives. The reason for this lies mainly in the weakness of the post-war Italian trade union movement until the watershed of 1969.

The late 1960s marked a profound change in the nature of employer–employee relations in general, laying the foundations for a period that has been described as an 'industrial citizenship', in which employees, at least in large-scale concerns, enjoyed a variety of legal protections and rights to consultation. The legal framework for this era was provided by two main reforms:

1 The Workers' Statute, based on agreements that had been thrashed out with the employers on the shop floor, was enacted into law. This gave trade unions the legal right to a presence in the workplace. The unions were also given the right to establish works councils.
2 The *scala mobile*, introduced in 1946, was reformed, linking price rises to wages in a way that increased the egalitarian tendency of wages, as the same wage rise was given to all employees, irrespective of age, sex, skill or sector, and appeared automatically in wage packets every three months. The pay indexation system had an enormous symbolic and real impact, giving security and protection in periods of high inflation.

The legal protection of rights and wages increased the power and confidence of workers and their representatives. Management was now called to consult employees in the newly established institution of workplace representation, the works councils. Workers' representatives enjoyed considerable resources and courtesies such as paid time off normal duties for trade union work and office facilities. Employees were also given time off work to attend meetings of their trade unions, which could be held on the premises.

The 1980s and the decline of the trade unions

By the end of the golden decade of the 1970s, the power of the trade unions was noticeably in decline again. A large part of the reason for this was that increasingly they no longer represented the typical worker: indeed, there was no longer a typical worker. The large-scale factory where predominantly male workforces carry out routine tasks on heavy machinery to make standardised goods is not necessarily the most efficient way of organising production, especially as the large concentration of workers doing essentially similar jobs makes it vulnerable to strikes and other forms of industrial action. Technologies and organisational techniques allowing a decentralisation of production to smaller units were now being developed with increasing urgency in the advanced industrial societies and rising productivity in manufacturing was allowing further shifts towards the traditionally decentralised service sector.

The consequences of these processes for the trade union confederations were very large. Not only was their natural membership of blue-collar workers in large industries reduced, but also autonomous trade unions, operating independently from and in competition with the big three confederations, have become an increasingly important phenomenon. The multitude of independent unions, now found in many sectors of the economy, offered professional and white-collar employees, especially, a new possibility of wage differentiation and thus had a strong appeal in those sectors that felt they had lost out in the general Italian trend to wage egalitarianism.

Following a highly symbolic defeat of a 1980 strike at FIAT, the trade unions appeared increasingly ineffective in their efforts to defend or improve the terms and conditions of work at company or national level. An important illustration of the weakening of the trade unions is given by their inability to defend the *scala mobile* wage indexation system, which was first watered down in the 1980s and then, after a referendum, finally abolished in 1992.

Trade union and employee rights in the 1990s

But trade unions in Italy still retained powerful support from
the employees who had benefited from the achievements of
the 1970s. While they were not able to defend the *scala mobile*,
with its implications of increasing wage equality, they have
been more successful in defending other rights, protections
and benefits. Unlike the trade unions in the UK after the
miners' strike of 1984–5, Italian trade unions have made
something of a comeback from the doldrums of the 1980s.

In July 1993, a central agreement was negotiated between
unions, employers and government. This historic tripartite
pact pushed forward the reshaping of workplace representation.
Incomes policy is now developed in meetings of representatives of employers, workers and government. The schedule of
meetings is set to coincide with key moments in the government's economic decision-making process, giving them a
timely impact on government thinking. The agreement sim-
plified the bargaining system, replacing the decentralised and
rather chaotic system with two levels, national and company.
Company bargaining cannot reverse agreements made at the
national level and mainly concerns consultation over the
introduction of new technologies and working practices and
their effects on health, safety, working conditions and equality
of opportunity. The agreement also firmed up new institutions
of employee representation at company level.

The agreement also contained several important concessions that employers had been demanding, for example
allowing the use of temporary agency workers who could be
brought into the workforce as needed. However, this flexibility
is tightly regulated, to prevent the destruction of secure jobs.

It will take some time for the reforms to bed in, especially in
the light of the new unpredictability of Italian politics following the collapse of the traditional parties, after which Italy has
experienced unelected 'technical' governments, the centre-
right administration of Silvio Berlusconi and Romano Prodi's
centre-left 'Olive Tree' government. As noted in chapter 2,

major constitutional reforms are also on the way and the effects that these may have on employer–employee relationships cannot be known.

One possibility is a move in the direction of the German model of industrial relations, in which powerful, disciplined and centralised trade unions negotiate framework sectoral contracts and employees are offered significant opportunities of consultation and participation at company level. Movement in this direction is seen, for example, in the increasing convergence of the big three trade union confederations, which are under a common threat from the autonomous unions, and in the merger of two main employers' associations. A continued strong voice for trade unions is made more likely by the fact that Communist Refoundation, the left-wing breakaway group from the former PCI, can hold the balance of power in Italy's multi-party system.

On the other hand, even the leadership of the centre-left believes that Italian competitiveness depends on increasing the flexibility of the labour market and is envious of the UK's Labour government, whose inheritance from Margaret Thatcher included a much weakened trade union movement.

Women and the State: at home and in work

Family law

Until 1975, family law in Italy was based largely on the provisions of the Fascist penal code of 1930 and the civil code of 1942. Although the 1948 constitution established women's 'moral and legal equality' within marriage, it also left the details of the implementation of this equality to the existing ordinary law, in other words mostly the aforementioned Fascist codes. In line with the patriarchal ideology of Fascism, the laws enshrined a rigid and hierarchical ideal of the family, in which the husband had the right to control the behaviour and activities of the wife. The civil code restricted the rights of women to remarry after annulment or widowhood (the only ways in which marriage could be dissolved). The family wealth, including any dowry brought to the marriage by the woman, was to be administered by the husband, who also retained any revenues from it. The father had authority over the children, which meant among other things that a woman left on her own with her children could find herself on very insecure legal ground when trying to arrange for their education and care. The 1975 Family Law Act finally established parity between the marriage partners and removed legal discriminations against children born out of wedlock.

Divorce and abortion

The issues of divorce and abortion provided the arenas for some of the most hard-fought contests in Italian political history. The idea of legal divorce, granted by the secular State, was a major challenge to the Catholic concept of the indissolubility of marriage and to the Church's privileged role in the ordering of family life. The sensitivity of the issue was such that even the PCI was loathe to raise it, for fear that open debate would be harmful to its strategy of reconciliation with the DC. Discussion of divorce emerged only from the 1960s and then mainly as a response to the situation of the many 'white widows', left alone to care for their children while their emigrant husbands often set up new families abroad. It has been estimated that there were as many as two and a half million such separated couples by 1969. In 1971, a law allowing for legal divorce was passed. But even as the parliamentary procedures for its passage began, the anti-divorce lobby had swung into action. Paradoxically, in fact, the divorce law was a strong motivation for the enactment of the constitutional provisions for referendums. Foreseeing the final passage of the bill, anti-divorce forces took immediate action to push through a law enabling referendums, in the hope that one could then be used to repeal the divorce law. However, in a crushing blow to the Church and militant Catholicism, the Italian people voted in the 1974 referendum to retain access to divorce.

From then on, access to referendums to repeal laws, in part or in whole, became a major weapon of the left and especially of the small but active Radical Party in the 1970s.

Abortion, too, had been illegal since the penal code of 1930, which made it a crime punishable by a sentence of between two and five years for both the woman concerned and the practitioner. The impact of this law on women was compounded by the fact that the advertisement, sale and distribution of contraception were also illegal, while Catholic domination of the education system meant that formal sex education was virtually unavailable. Illegal abortion, with all its connotations, thus became a form of contraception after the act and was a normal experience for many women for generations.

A law permitting abortion, on certain conditions, was passed despite the abstention of the DC in 1978, during the government of national unity supported by the PCI. However, abortion was still difficult to obtain. The law allowed for conscientious objection to involvement in abortion and many doctors feared damage to their careers if they opted to perform them, since the DC tended to dominate hospital hierarchies.

Women at work

Official rates of female participation in the labour force in Italy are below the European average, although women in Italy, as elsewhere, tend to be disproportionately engaged in irregular forms of work and in the submerged economy. Perhaps partly as a result of the rather low proportion of women in official, full-time employment, and the consequent predominance of men in the trade union movement, laws promoting equality of opportunity for women are few.

Early legislation tended to exclude women from certain types of work (they could not teach history, economics or philosophy in the schools, for example) and confirm them in the role of motherhood. Under Fascism, a series of laws made (unpaid) maternity leave compulsory. This legislation was repealed in the immediate post-war period, following a campaign by women trade unionists. The new law, passed in 1950, gave women an entitlement to maternity leave which was among the most generous in Europe and the law has been progressively reformed in women's favour since then.

Although the 1950 law was a response to a trade union campaign, it should be noted that the bill that was finally approved was presented by a senior DC MP and that resistance to it was not as strong as might have been expected. Laws protecting the pregnant woman and, perhaps especially, her child have a long history in Italy and result from desires to reinforce women's role as mothers and to ensure the production of a new generation of healthy Italians as well as from real concern for women and the choices that face them. In fact, while paid maternity leave is obviously fundamental in ensuring equality of opportunity, it is not on its own sufficient, especially as the financial obligations the law places on the employer may be a disincentive to the employment of women.

During the 1970s, as women began to find a strong voice within the trade union movement and more generally in the feminist movement, there was some improvement in the framework of laws and institutions that could allow women to make real choices concerning their careers. For example, a law was enacted providing for the establishment of nurseries and their administration by the regions. A landmark piece of legislation came in 1977, when the Equal Treatment Act ended legal discrimination on the basis of sex in the workplace. The law imposed equal pay for equal work and gave trade unions sometimes uncomfortable responsibilities, such as deciding whether certain jobs are too heavy or dangerous for women. However, this law responded to European Community directives. Its application has not been widespread and women have rarely used the law to bring employers to arbitration.

Women at home and at work: a summary

The late development in Italy of the legal instruments and practical institutions that help equalise the opportunities of the two sexes is mainly explained by the ideology of the Church and its impact on the main parties. In this ideology, the woman as wife and mother carries the central responsibility for the health and welfare of the family. With the guidance and support of the Church, she will care for the sick and ageing and be active in the Christian education of the young. Fathers, by the same token, have the duty to work to provide for the present and future economic needs of the family. Any interference within these roles by the State might only serve to undermine the family by removing essential functions from it and loosening the bonds that hold it together. What is more, the Church played a very central role in the delivery of education and social services through its own schools and its special status in State education, and through its network of charitable associations giving help to the needy. The extension of secular, State-run institutions into these realms would have helped women combine paid work with responsibilities at home, but would have constituted a great threat to the authority of the Church. The DC needed the continued support of the Church and was loathe to pursue policies that would be unwelcome to its powerful ally.

The PCI, for its part, never provided a consistent counter theme to the ideology of the sanctity of the family. It was terrified of laying itself open to accusations that it was anti-family, and pursued a course of accommodation with Catholic teaching as part of its strategy of alliance with the DC, an alliance it justified by pointing to similarities between Catholic and Communist notions of social solidarity. From the formative years of the Republic, the family was presented in Communist literature as 'the original nucleus on which the citizens and the State must depend for the social and moral renewal of Italy' (*Rinascità*, 1 September 1946).

There were, of course, significant divergences between Catholic and Communist views on women and the family. Nevertheless, the sensitivity of the PCI and many Communist women to Catholic concerns regarding the sanctity of the family and women's natural centrality to it meant that Italian women never had the support of a political party committed to thoroughgoing reform in the direction of equal opportunity.

The DC, of course, no longer exists, although its old bases of support are regrouping behind new political forces. It remains to be seen whether the Catholic Church can retain its influence on the ordering of family life, especially in view of the increasing secularisation of Italian society.

Further reading

Ascoli, U. 'The Italian Welfare State: Between Incrementalism and Rationalism', in Friedmann, N. G., et al. (eds), *Modern Welfare States: A Comparative View of Trends and Prospects*, Brighton (1987).

Caldwell, L. *Italian Family Matters: Women, Politics and Legal Reform*, London (1991).

Ferrera, M. 'Italy', in Flora, P. (ed.), *Growth to Limits: The European Welfare State Since World War Two*, Berlin (1987).

7

Terrorism, organised crime and corruption

Introduction

As a theatre for political intrigue, clandestine operations, conspiracies and plots, Italy has been unmatched in post-war Western Europe. Mysteries abound, as do theories to explain them. However, many commentators agree that the occult operations that have characterised the struggle for power in Italy can nearly all be linked in one way or another to the existence in Italy of the strongest Communist movement in the Western world. The strength of the PCI, especially during the period of its increasing influence, the 1960s and 1970s, made Italy a focus for Western, and especially US, fears. In some theories, covert operations intended to shore up the crumbling defences against Communism resulted in the construction of a shadowy alternative authority which sometimes overruled that of the formal and constitutional State.

Political polarisation

We have already seen that Italy is a deeply polarised society, in which extremes of right and left have thrived in the absence of an acceptable, reform-minded political class of centrist persuasion capable of accommodating and reconciling the different strands of political tradition in a coherent programme of change. Until very recently, persons of a centre-left persuasion have not had effective political representation in government, as the main party of the left was the PCI, which was excluded from government. The linchpin of the PCI's strategy to achieve representation in government was to pursue an alliance with the DC. One result of this strategy was a gradual move to the right, which left the PCI's own left wing increasingly resentful. This led to the emergence within the party of vociferous left factions, such as the 1968 Manifesto group (which was expelled in 1969) and more recently Communist Refoundation, which split to the left in 1991 after the PCI changed its name to the PDS.

The PCI's move to the right also increased the attractions of extra-parliamentary politics. This space has been filled since the 1960s with numerous far-left parties, groupings and social movements. Fragmentation and rancour on the left were increased in the 1970s when the PCI, anxious not to be associated with the left movements and keen to show that it could restore law and order, clamped down not only on terrorism, but on social and civil rights protest in general.

At the other end of the spectrum, profoundly conservative forces have also continued to exist in Italian society, often at the very heart of the State machinery. Elements that are nostalgic for an imagined past of an ordered, hierarchical and patriarchal society are present among the Church, the military and the secret services, as well as within the judiciary and public administration. A number of factors have facilitated the perpetuation of these backward-looking, conservative forces. One of these is the special place held by the Catholic Church in Italian society. Although there is no inevitable association between Catholicism and right-wing ideologies, forms of authoritarian nostalgia, as well as the Church's possession of very considerable wealth, have often, historically, linked it to the right. For some elements within the Church, processes of modernisation are a threat to the very foundations of its authority. There are still those who yearn for the rigidly hierarchical society of the past, in which the priesthood interpreted the word of God to the faithful and the teachings of the Church were unchallenged. While some within the Church have responded with sensitivity to demands for a democratic and open society based on equality of opportunity, for others secularisation is a direct and terrible threat to the natural order of society.

The persistence of extreme conservatism in Italy was also facilitated by the incomplete break with Fascism. The purge of Fascists from vital functions in society after the war was very partial and strong Fascistic residues remained, especially within the military and public administration. Fascist ideology was given permanence and a nucleus around which to build support by the neo-Fascist MSI, a political party formed from the remnants of the Italian Social Republic, established by Mussolini in 1943 in Salò. The leadership of the MSI has never rejected its Fascist past, even since its transformation into the National Alliance (Alleanza Nazionale, AN) in 1994–5. The party consistently attracted electoral support of around 5 per cent throughout the post-war period, although, like the PCI, it was excluded from government until the collapse of the traditional parties afforded it a new opportunity.

Given the coexistence of powerful currents of left- and right-wing ideology, it is unsurprising that extremism has often found expression in violent and illegal forms. And given the influence of extreme conservatism within some sectors of the establishment, this expression has sometimes taken place in occult collusion with segments of the public powers.

The 'years of the bullet'

Tensions between left and right reached a climax during the 1970s, a decade that has gone down in history as the 'years of the bullet' (*anni di piombo*). It seemed that the fabric of Italian society was being torn apart, as mounting civil unrest was punctuated by terrorist outrages from left and right.

The right feared the seemingly inexorable march forward of the left, punctuated by the inclusion of the PSI in government since 1963, the consolidation of trade union power since 1969, the increasing electoral support for the PCI, peaking in 1976, the governments of national unity of 1976–9, which gave the PCI the status of a governing party, and the widespread networks of youth and social protest from the late 1960s.

Many believed that conservative elements within the establishment were pursuing a strategy of tension, in which social tensions were deliberately fomented so that the re-establishment of order by an authoritarian regime would be welcomed. This strategy was in fact used by the Greek colonels before their military coup.

Red terrorism

The 1970s saw a sustained terrorist campaign by the Red Brigades (Brigate Rosse, BR) that continued into the 1980s. This group theorised that their use of violent, armed struggle would provoke a right-wing backlash. The true nature of the State as a purely coercive force would thus be revealed and it would be overthrown by the insurgent masses. The BR were not the only left-wing terrorists operating in Italy in the 1970s and 1980s. Other groups, born from disagreements with the BR over strategy, although ultimately engaging in similar activities, were the Armed Proletarian Nuclei and Front Line (Prima Linea).

The BR emerged from the early 1970s against a backdrop of widespread and generally legal struggle by revolutionary groups like Lotta Continua (the Struggle Goes On) and Potere Operaio (Workers' Power). Some of the Red Brigadists had in fact been in these groups. At the beginning, the BR targeted right-wing trade unionists, managers and foremen, mainly in Milan. These 'collaborators' were subjected to beatings or had their cars burnt. By the mid-1970s, the old guard of the BR

had largely been taken out of action by anti-terrorist operations and new, even more ruthless recruits took their place.
From around 1977, the BR engaged in a campaign of kidnap
and murder that would ultimately involve police, magistrates,
journalists and university lecturers. However, the authorities
remained firm in their refusal to make any concession to the
terrorists' demands.

The height of BR notoriety was reached in March 1978,
during the presentation of the second government of national
unity that involved the PCI in the formulation of policy. The
red terrorists kidnapped Aldo Moro, a prominent DC politician
who was the main interlocutor between the DC and the PCI.
His chauffeur and police escort were killed in the attack and
Moro was held captive for nearly two months before being
murdered. During the time of Moro's imprisonment, a debate
raged in society at large. Should the State negotiate with the
kidnappers to secure his release, as Moro requested in letters
to his family and colleagues, or would any form of compromise
encourage the terrorists to further outrages? The latter argu-
ment, to which the PCI strongly subscribed, prevailed. Moro
was killed on 9 May 1978 and his body was found in a car left,
symbolically, mid-way between the headquarters of the DC
and PCI.

The firm stance against terrorism probably paid off. Although the killings and other actions continued well into
the 1980s, the red terrorists were increasingly isolated as the
belief that Italy was experiencing a potentially revolutionary
moment was shown to be unfounded. A major factor in the
eradication of left-wing terrorism in Italy was a controversial
law offering reduced sentences to terrorists who were willing
to repent and inform on their erstwhile colleagues. As a
result of this law, a number of terrorists received extremely
light sentences in return for their collaboration. A key
figure in acquiring the intelligence used to break up the
remaining BR columns was the Carabiniere general, Carlo
Alberto Dalla Chiesa, who coordinated the anti-terrorist
offensive.

'Black' or right-wing terrorism

The 1970s were also punctuated by a series of outrages ultimately found to be the work of the extreme right, which had become increasingly nervous about the advances of the left.

In December 1969, Italy's 'hot autumn' was working itself out with the agreement of a national contract that was greeted as a very significant victory for the trade unions. That very month, a bomb exploded in a bank in Milan's Piazza Fontana. Sixteen people died in the attack and eighty-eight were wounded. Another two bombs of same type went off in Rome, where there were injuries but no deaths. The death toll of right-wing terrorism continued to rise in the years that followed. In 1970, a train was derailed in the south, killing six. In May 1974, a bomb exploded during an anti-Fascist demonstration in Brescia. The device had been planted in a rubbish bin under a portico where a number of people had gathered to shelter from the rain. Eight died in the attack and a further 102 were injured. Later in that year the express train Italicus was bombed, with the loss of twelve lives. In August 1980, a bomb left in Bologna station exploded, killing eighty-five people.

In a pattern that was to become commonplace, police investigations after the bomb in Piazza Fontana focused on anarchist groupings and some leading figures on the left were rounded up by police. One fell to his death from the fourth floor of the police station where he was being kept for questioning. The official explanation of his death was that he had committed suicide, presumably tormented by guilt. Six years later, however, the courts were to clear him of any involvement in the outrages.

It emerged that evidence not initially pursued by the police pointed to an extreme right grouping based in the Veneto region. One of the neo-Fascists implicated in the bombings turned out to be in close contact with a colonel in the secret services. Gradually, a sustained effort of investigative journalism was building up a picture of a densely interwoven network connecting the secret services and extreme right groups.

Many sectors of the press and the political parties of opposition were by now calling for a thorough independent investigation of the activities of the secret services. Not only was this not forthcoming, but an establishment cover-up seemed to be in process. Access to secret-service files was denied to magistrates investigating the Piazza Fontana bombing and the Supreme Court used its powers to delay and relocate the trial. In 1975, as the Milan magistrates were in the process of interrogating the heads of the secret services, responsibility for the investigations was transferred from Milan to Rome, where the officers could expect a more sympathetic attitude. In 1981, three neo-Fascists, including a colonel from the secret services, were sentenced to life imprisonment for the Piazza Fontana bombing, but were later cleared on appeal. All in all, despite years of trials and retrials, only a handful of right-wing terrorists have been convicted and sentenced.

Right-wing terror emerged again in the early 1990s. In May 1993, a car bomb went off outside the famous Uffizi gallery in Florence, killing the museum's caretaker, his wife and daughters. Over that summer, bombs also damaged a number of ancient churches in Rome. For the first time, the targets were primarily cultural. The new outrages followed the collapse of the traditional parties and the disgracing of large part of the political class that had for so long retained the reins of power. Small wonder, then, that many theorised a return to the strategy of tension, a warning, from the powers within and behind the old regime, that they would not easily give up their position of dominance. These suspicions were only reinforced when, a few days after the Rome bombings, Prime Minister Carlo Azeglio Ciampi sacked the chiefs of the two secret-service organisations and placed them under his own command.

The De Lorenzo and Borghese affairs

In the 1970s, evidence began to emerge that a right-wing strategy of tension may have been backed up with concrete plans for the seizure of power and the establishment of an authoritarian regime. It appeared that plans for a military putsch had in fact existed and in one case there had even been a fumbled attempt to seize power.

Giovanni De Lorenzo was the chief of the Carabinieri and a former head of military intelligence. In the summer of 1964, during the negotiation of a new centre-left government, he finalised a plan for what could only be interpreted as a coup d'état. The plan, code-named Solo, was detailed, involving the arrest and detention of large numbers of leading politicians, the occupation of prefectures, the take-over of national radio and television networks and the seizure of headquarters of left parties.

The plan was never put into action and the majority of the parliamentary commission set up to enquire into it concluded that it was essentially defensive, to be set in motion only in the case of danger to the institutions of the Republic. But whether its intention was offensive or defensive, the plan was discomforting, suggesting that elements within the State would be prepared, under conditions of real or imagined threat, to bypass democratic procedures and establish a right-wing government by force. The plan became public knowledge through the investigative efforts of two journalists in the late 1960s. In 1970, a judicial investigation found that De Lorenzo had acted against the law and the constitution. But since he was by this time an MP (he was elected as a Monarchist and then swapped allegiance to the neo-fascist MSI), he was afforded parliamentary immunity and escaped prosecution.

Another incident implicating the Italian secret services in right-wing authoritarian plots occurred in December 1970. Prince Junio Valerio Borghese, who had been a naval commander in the Fascist Republic of Salò, made a rather farcical attempt to overthrow the government and replace it with a military regime. With a small band of men, he actually succeeded in occupying the Ministry of the Interior for a few hours. Evidence later accumulated that Borghese had close connections within the secret services and the military. In 1974, judicial investigations implicated the head of the intelligence services, General Vito Miceli, of complicity in the plot. Miceli was a member of the secret Masonic lodge Propaganda 2, described below. Eventually, four generals, including Miceli, were brought to trial, but all were acquitted.

Propaganda 2

In 1981, the existence of a powerful Masonic lodge known as Propaganda 2, or P2, was uncovered following a police raid on the office of its grand master, Licio Gelli. The raid followed investigations into the activities of a Sicilian tax lawyer, Michele Sindona, who had a web of banking interests in Italy, the USA and elsewhere. Sindona also had intimate relations with the Vatican and through these contacts had met a number of senior DC politicians, including Giulio Andreotti. Sindona had fled to the USA in the early 1970s as investigators closed in on him in Italy. When his US banking interests also ran into trouble, he arranged for his own kidnap and under the cover of this returned secretly to Italy.

One of the contacts he made while in hideout in Sicily was with Licio Gelli. It was this link that the magistrates were investigating when, in March 1981, they came across evidence concerning P2.

In Gelli's office, the magistrates discovered a suitcase of papers, containing photocopies and original documents relating to illegal financial operations. The most startling discovery, however, was the membership list of P2. The list revealed that literally hundreds of prominent people were members of the lodge, including cabinet ministers, MPs, politicians of all the parties except the PCI and Radicals, army personnel, industrialists, bankers, magistrates, editors, civil servants and much of the leadership of the secret services, including their heads. Silvio Berlusconi, whose right-wing alliance was to win the 1994 elections, was also among the names.

The scandal that broke out after the list was made public was such that the Prime Minister, Arnaldo Forlani, was forced to resign. He was replaced by the Republican Giovanni Spadolini, the first non-DC politician to hold that office since 1945.

Another mystery relating to P2 was the death of Roberto Calvi, nicknamed God's banker for the extensive links of his Ambrosiano bank with the Vatican's Institute for Religious Works. Calvi was a member of P2, had been Sindona's partner in many deals and was considered the financial arm of Gelli's P2. In May 1981, at the same time as the P2 membership list was released, Calvi was arrested on charges relating to illegal financial operations. He spent six weeks in prison, during which time he claimed he had channelled large sums of money to the PSI. Calvi was later released pending his appeal and returned to head the Ambrosiano. Less than one year later, on the eve of the collapse of the Ambrosiano, he was found hanging under Blackfriars Bridge in London, his pockets stuffed with stones. The Masonic symbolism, particularly of the name of the bridge and the stones, led many in Italy to believe that Calvi had not died by his own hand but had been silenced. For some, Calvi had been murdered by agents of the political parties who had received financing through the banker's offices. The public voicing of this suspicion by the leader of the Radical Party was not met by any legal measures. For others, Calvi had been controlled by the Mafia and it was here that his killers should be sought. The London inquest first returned a verdict of suicide, although a second inquest returned an open verdict.

Sindona and Calvi had both been vital elements in P2, Sindona mainly for his contacts in the USA and Calvi for his money.

The purpose of P2

For many, P2 was a sort of invisible power within the State. It appeared that Gelli was at the centre of a right-wing, anti-Communist network linking important figures within the establishment. But what was it actually for? For its members, the Masonic network probably offered reciprocal support in obtaining and keeping important positions in society. Gelli, as the holder of the lodge's records (voluminous files and taped conversations with the rich and powerful), gained power over his numerous contacts: perhaps he was acting only on his own behalf. Certainly, the lodge was too dispersed and loosely organised to have directly orchestrated a military coup.

One objective that has been ascribed to P2 was to use propaganda to lay the bases for the establishment of a presidential regime. The centralisation of power, together with control over the media and the constraint of the judiciary and its sprinkling of dangerously independent magistrates, was an attractive idea to those who feared the apparent onward march of the left. One immediate aim of the lodge's closest associates was control over Italy's best-known newspaper, the *Corriere della Sera*, which it had won by the early 1980s. In this period, in fact, the newspaper printed uncritical commentaries on Gelli's activities and publicised the grand master's views on constitutional reform and his preference for a government led by Bettino Craxi and with an important role for Giulio Andreotti. A parliamentary commission set up to investigate P2 heard evidence of its involvement with right-wing terrorist groups and particularly with the Borghese group, whose 1970 plot the lodge is alleged to have helped conceal.

The Spadolini government made the fight against occult powers a main plank of its governmental programme. P2 was declared dissolved and high-ranking P2 army personnel were removed from their posts. However, calls from the President of the Republic, Sandro Pertini, for the sacking of politicians in P2 came to nothing.

After a long period in hiding, Gelli was captured attempting to withdraw money from a Swiss bank. Remarkably, he escaped from prison before he could be extradited, but has since been recaptured, and in 1994 he was sentenced to seventeen years in prison.

The Mafia

The Mafia originated in the Sicilian countryside in the mid-nineteenth century. The class of elite tenant farmers, who administered the great estates on behalf of absentee land-owners and also invested in the land they leased, wanted armed protection for their property and family, and the Mafia formed to offer them this. The Mafia, then, was not originally a society or organisation. Its members were typically small landowners, tenant farmers and small businessmen, especially merchants, while the use of violence was delegated to gangs of youths who gained status and advancement in a society that held very little opportunity for a poor young man.

During the period of the liberal regime, from 1860 to the advent of Fascism, the new Italian State granted the Mafia a virtual blank cheque to uphold order in large areas of southern Calabria and western Sicily. Toleration of the Mafia, and even collusion with it, have marked every political regime in place in the south from then at least until the collapse of the traditional parties of power in 1993.

The Mafia was weakened but by no means eradicated under Fascism, as Mussolini had many lower-ranking members rounded up and imprisoned: alternatives to his authority were not to be tolerated. However, much of the Mafia, and especially its more powerful elements, were able to adapt to the regime and camouflage themselves within it, often joining the Fascist National Party.

The Allied invasion ended Fascism in the south, but actually promoted the Mafia. From 1943 to 1945, under the Anglo-American military government that followed the Allied invasion, known Mafiosi were nominated as mayors of a number of towns and leading Italo-American Mafiosi were allowed to return to Italy. The US, especially, feared disturbing the systems of authority they found, lest their removal led to anarchy or Communism.

The Italian State that replaced the Allied authority also preferred coexistence with the Mafia to an attempt to eradicate it. At least initially, this was because the Mafia was a valuable ally in upholding the power of the landowners of the great estates. In fact, in the widespread rural insurrections of 1948–50 that seemed to bring Italy to the brink of civil war, the Mafia was a useful instrument for the forceful discipline of the insurgent peasants. Later on the Mafia became useful to some southern-based politicians, especially in the DC, for the role it could play in marshalling the vote in the south.

The rural bases of the Mafia began to disappear in the 1960s, as waves of emigrants left the south altogether while others transferred to the cities. However, the Mafia survived the transition by moving its activities to the growing urban centres, where it concentrated on the commerce of drugs. Various estimates of the proceeds of Mafia drug sales by the late 1970s and early 1980s range from $10 billion to $750 billion a year. Even were the lower estimate more accurate, it would bracket Mafia profits, from the drug trade alone, with those of the US-based multinational ITT.

Mafia and Mafia-type protection rackets and extortion have had devastating effects on the southern economy. It is impossible to estimate the amount of investment that has been lost to the south because of Mafia activities through the scaring off or squeezing out of legitimate enterprise.

A scholar of the Mafia, Pino Arlacchi (see further reading), has pointed out that Mafia enterprises enjoy considerable advantages over their non-Mafia counterparts. Because of their readiness to use violence and intimidation, the Mafia enterprises can acquire supplies at reduced prices and are not subject to normal competition in securing orders and contracts for products. The Mafia-run business can impose high productivity and low wages through an authoritarian organisation of work – protest by the workers would be ill-advised indeed. Mafia enterprises also have little difficulty in finding financing to expand or diversify, given that they can rely on such unorthodox sources of financing as profits from drugs and arms trafficking. Of course, Mafia enterprises are exposed to competition from other Mafia enterprises. This competition leads to an escalating cycle of coercion and violence as rival outfits battle to secure advantage.

The political power of the Mafia

The Mafia gains its political power mainly from its ability to control the vote in the south. In 1992, a journalist claimed that a full 10 per cent of the vote there was under the direct control of the Mafia and another 20 per cent under indirect control. (Many believed that their ballot paper could be identified and that retribution would follow a wrong vote.) Given the tight electoral mathematics of Italy's multi-party system, this portion of the vote was clearly a necessary – though ultimately not sufficient – condition for the continuation in power of the DC. Long-standing conjectures of direct links between the Mafia and the summits of political power have recently become the subject of formal enquiry and public debate through what is perhaps Italy's most extraordinary trial to date.

In the summer of 1994, Giulio Andreotti, Italy's best-known and most senior politician, was arrested on Mafia-related charges. Andreotti had been Prime Minister of Italy on no less than seven occasions and had held senior jobs in another twenty-two cabinets. In a trial that is still in process at the time of writing, he stands accused of offering political and judicial protection to the Mafia and, in another case, of ordering the murder of a journalist who had uncovered evidence of the alleged links of the Mafia with political power. A key witness for the prosecution is the repented Mafioso Baldassare Di Maggio. Di Maggio claims that during a visit to Palermo in 1987, Andreotti received a kiss on both cheeks from the Mafia boss of bosses, Toto Riina. The bestowal of such a kiss is charged with symbolism, signifying authority over the person who receives it.

The anti-Mafia struggle

Resistance to the Mafia has been courageous, but until recently largely isolated. Given the tremendous economic and political resources that the Mafia and similar clans enjoy, this is less surprising than it may seem at first sight. Until the 1990s, the political will to defeat the Mafia was tenuous, for obvious reasons. The Mafia, after all, was helpful in delivering the vote and even if only a minority of DC politicians benefited directly from its electoral activities, the capacity for survival of the governing coalition as a whole would be further undermined by any loss of vote. Thus anti-Mafia legislation remained blocked in parliament and the deployment of extra resources and trained personnel to deal with the problem was resisted. When suspected Mafiosi were charged, trials were often delayed and transferred by acquiescent elements in the judiciary. There was little, either, by the way of a genuine popular will to defeat the Mafia. The criminal associations were, after all, a source of jobs and money and helped channel resources to the south in return for organising the local vote. Even the Church has been largely acquiescent, recognising the important role the Mafia played in the continued electoral success of its favoured party.

There are noble exceptions to this general rule. General Alberto Dalla Chiesa, the Carabiniere officer who had played an important role in the struggle against terrorism, was sent by the government to Palermo to lead the fight against the Mafia. A few months later, in September 1982, Dalla Chiesa and his wife were assassinated by the Mafia. Following the murder and the public outcry that followed it, some more extra resources were allocated to the fight against the Mafia. The post of anti-Mafia commissioner was created and given wide powers to investigate. Soon after that, new legislation made it illegal to belong to the Mafia, permitted the investigation of the banking activities of suspects and authorised the confiscation of bank accounts. But these measures were still insufficient to release the south from the stranglehold of the criminal associations.

Since the early 1990s, however, the political and popular will to rid the south of the scourge of the Mafia and its sister organisations seems to have re-emerged. The revitalisation of the struggle against the Mafia coincided with the degeneration and collapse of the traditional parties of power. June 1992 saw the biggest anti-Mafia demonstration in Sicily's history. The demonstration, organised by the trade union confederations, was called in response to the murder of the anti-Mafia magistrate Giovanni Falcone, his wife and three bodyguards. While the mass demonstration did not have immediate effect (Falcone's successor, Paolo Borsellino, was killed with his bodyguards by a car bomb just two months later), it seemed to embody a new mood.

An important factor in turning the tide in the struggle against the Mafia has been the introduction of more stringent anti-Mafia measures, allowing confiscation of Mafia property and inducements for Mafiosi to repent and inform. Since the early 1990s, a steady stream of Mafiosi have given evidence in return for reduced sentences and protection from reprisal by their erstwhile colleagues. Over the past years, thousands of suspected Mafiosi have been arrested, mostly as a result of information from ex-Mafiosi who have repented on the promise of being giving police protection, money, new homes and new identities. This has led to some concerns, not only about the lenient treatment meted out but also about the reliability of information obtained in this way. Informing to the authorities may, of course, be a way of settling old scores.

However, it would be overly sanguine to conclude that the Mafia is definitely on the run in southern Italy. Poverty and unemployment, the material bases for the Mafia's expansion, still exist and it is not impossible that organised crime will find political protectors again. The Mafia seemed to experience a renewed period of confidence in the latter part of 1994, during the brief right-wing government headed by Silvio Berlusconi, when headquarters of anti-Mafia parties were burnt down and some anti-Mafia public officials suffered retributions and threats, such as the classic severed calf's head on the doorstep. In the aftermath of the general elections of 1994, which ended in victory for the right-wing alliance, there were allegations that the Mafia was performing electoral services for Berlusconi's party Forza Italia!, just as they had for the now defunct DC.

Further reading

On Mafia enterprise see Arlacchi, P. 'The Mafioso: From Man of Honour to Entrepreneur', *New Left Review*, November–December, No. 118 (1979).

On 'red' and 'black' terrorism and the involvement of the secret services see particularly Ginsborg, P. *A History of Contemporary Italy: Society and Politics 1943–1988*, London (1990), and Spotts, F. and Weiser, T. *Italy: A Difficult Democracy*, Cambridge (1986) (especially chapter 9, 'Dangers to the State'): both are cited in the bibliography.

8

Italy in the 1990s

Introduction

The 1990s are extraordinary times for Italian democracy. Uniquely in a previously stable Western democracy, all the main parties of the traditional party system have collapsed under the weight of corruption or have undergone radical transformation, new parties have emerged and the relationships among the new or transformed parties have changed, resulting in a major mutation of the whole party system. Following radical reform of the electoral rules in 1993 and the election of fresh personnel to government, the passage to the Second Republic has been widely acclaimed.

The particracy of the First Republic was rooted in inter- and intra-party competition for public resources that could be used to benefit 'clients' in society and thus enhance electoral support and personal careers in the parties. This chapter will assess the claim that a new, Second Republic is emerging from the ashes of the First.

The evidence of change

A rapid review of some of the major changes in the Italian political landscape suggests there is some foundation for the view that a major transition has taken place.

- Under pressure from the new electoral law of 1993, which replaced pure PR and introduced a mainly first-past-the-post system, the highly fragmented and ideologically divided multi-party system appears to be recoalescing into two major blocs, on the left and right of centre.
- Alternation between these blocs has already occurred. Silvio Berlusconi's right-wing coalition governed for seven months in 1994 and, after a period of 'technical' government, the left-of-centre coalition headed by Romano Prodi was elected in April 1996.
- By the 1994 election, it was fairly clear that Berlusconi would be the Prime Minister if the right won, although Gianfranco Fini, leader of the former neo-Fascists, was also a contender. By the 1996 election, fairly clear candidates for the premiership had emerged for both blocs. The electorate could thus vote for a Prime Minister, as well as a party.
- There has been some renewal of the personnel of parliament, the period 1992–4 seeing the biggest turnover of MPs since the election of the first Republican parliament in 1946.
- Despite resistance and modification, some legislation has been enacted to tackle the problem of systemic corruption. New regulations, for example governing the allocation of public contracts, are in place, some obsolete and non-useful public bodies have been abolished and some areas of the public administration have been reshaped.
- The process of selling off large parts of Italy's sprawling public sector, the rich source of so much clientelistic exchange, is under way.

At least on the face of it, the key conditions that sustained the rule of the parties have disappeared. The complacent DC dynasty that presided over endemic corruption has been discredited and abandoned. Voters have been able to judge a government on its merits and, finding it wanting, replace it with a different set of political leaders. Governments and potential governments are now in a position to set out their plans before elections, have them ratified by the electorate and stand accountable if they fail to implement them to the satisfaction of those who voted them in.

That is the optimistic view. More cynical observers suggest that many, if not most, of those with power within the old regime are still in place, inside and outside parliament, and that the culture of political exchange of votes for favours will not be uprooted just by tinkering with institutional arrangements.

It is early yet to judge. At this stage, it is possible to identify only the main trends in the restructuring of the party system and make a preliminary assessment of the performance so far of the governments that have alternated in office since 1994.

The emerging party system

As we saw in chapter 2, a massive reform campaign in the early 1990s led to the establishment in August 1993 of new electoral rules, by which most candidates are selected in single-member constituencies and elected on a first-past-the-post basis similar to that used in the UK. The new, more majoritarian electoral arrangements are set out on page 41.

A first-past-the-post system tends to force parties on the same side of the left–right divide to cooperate or even to form alliances. In theory, this should lead to a simplification of the party system and ultimately the emergence of two main moderate parties, both with the potential to gain a majority of the vote and govern alone.

The first test: the 1993 local elections

The first test of the new majoritarian electoral rules came in local elections concluded in December 1993. By and large, the parties that had survived the collapse of 1992–3 adjusted as expected to the new electoral rules. Two distinctive blocs or 'poles' were formed, and ideological messages were generally softened.

In the run up to the elections, the PDS was able to put together a not entirely harmonious Progressive Alliance including the hard left Communist Refoundation, the Greens, Network (a grouping of left Catholic anti-Mafia campaigners) and a new moderate party, Democratic Alliance. The PDS's replacement of the hammer and sickle symbol with a more neutral and environmentally friendly oak tree helped draw other parties into the alliance, despite the inevitable resentment about the dominant role of the former Communists. The smaller parties did not want to become the undergrowth surviving in the shade of the oak, but they knew they faced electoral extinction if they ran alone. But despite the bickering, especially over the allocation of constituency candidacies in safe seats among the component parts of the alliance, the breadth of the coalition was an early sign that the PDS could attract the support that would allow it to break out of the electoral ghetto in which its forerunner, the PCI, had long been trapped by anti-Communist sentiment.

At this stage, the right was less successful in overcoming its inherent ideological divisions and forming a convincing electoral coalition. The MSI attempted to broaden its appeal as a respectable party of the right, although it did not formally change its name (to the National Alliance) until its January 1995 congress. The Northern League softened its separatist rhetoric. However, the two parties could not countenance cooperation at this stage. The electoral appeal of the Northern League is based to a large extent on anti-southern sentiments: the party portrays a parasitic south leaching the profits of northern industriousness. The ultimate goal of its most radical wing is the secession of the north and the break-up of the Republic. The AN, on the other hand, is a right-wing nationalist party whose appeal is fundamentally based on national patriotism. An important part of its membership and support comes from the administrative machinery of the central State, whose death warrant would be signed by a major devolution of powers. However, the electorate of the Northern League is, for obvious reasons, largely confined to the north, while the

AN has its electoral heartland in the south. Because the two parties compete in different geographical areas, an alliance for the local elections was not absolutely necessary.

The overall results of the 1993 local elections (including elections held earlier in the year) were a victory for the left and confirmed the demise of the parties of the old coalition system. Out of 221 mayors elected, only nine were DC, while the PDS gained 103. This catastrophe signalled the end of the DC, not just as a dynasty, but as a party. In January 1994, it dissolved. Since then, two new parties have formed from its remnants. One reclaimed the historic name Italian Popular Party (Partito Popolare Italiano, PPI), the other calls itself the Christian Democratic Centre (Centro Cristiano Democratico). Centre fragments, such as the remnants of the DC and the Pact for Italy party that had emerged from the movement for electoral reform, have further complicated the process of forming two main right and left alliances.

The victory of the left in the local elections of 1993, however, did not reflect the natural choice of many voters. The result was skewed by the fact that only the PDS, smaller leftist parties, MSI and Northern League had survived the corruption scandals more or less intact, because they had never played a full part in the old ruling coalitions. Since a vote for the discredited parties of the old centre was mostly discounted, electors were generally faced with a choice between a candidate backed by the PDS, or a candidate backed by either the neo-Fascists or the populist and separatist Northern League. Many former centre voters probably voted for a candidate of the left as the lesser of two evils.

The 1994 general elections

In 1994 a general election was called to replace the interim 'technical' government led by Carlo Azeglio Ciampi, which had been brought in to preside over the unprecedented crisis of legitimisation and put the electoral reforms in place. The general election took place on 27–28 March 1994, just three months after the local elections.

In the early stages of the electoral campaigns, the left appeared as the likely winners. They were more unified than the right and their confidence had been buoyed by the victories in the local elections. However, given the historic electoral predominance of the centre and the profundity of the Catholic–Communist divide that had for so long kept the old PCI trapped under an electoral ceiling of around one-third of the vote, in retrospect it does not seem surprising that some new force should have swept in to claim the centre vote as its own.

The emergence of Forza Italia!

Silvio Berlusconi was a television mogul with the financial resources, the connections, the personal charm and above all the media influence to manufacture and sell a new political formation, purpose built to defeat the left, in the three months between the December local elections and the general elections of March 1994.

Where old certainties lay shattered, Berlusconi's smiling face from the small screen he dominated was a reassurance. After the national humiliation of the corruption scandals, he offered a dream of Italian rebirth on the Italian strong suit of entrepreneurial dynamism. His own rags-to-riches career seemed to embody a potent Italian dream of national transformation. With the sure instinct born of his media experience, Berlusconi baptised his creation Forza Italia! (Come on Italy!) and dubbed his followers the *Azurri*, or light blues, a reference to the national football strip. The new party adopted a stirring anthem: 'It's time to go, it's time to dare'. Thousands of Forza Italia! clubs were set up, and their presidents were charged 500,000 lire for kits containing propaganda material, a watch and a few pens. The best market-research talents of Berlusconi's company, Fininvest, were siphoned off into a new company, Diakron, which provided virtually continuous updates on the movement's surging support. Berlusconi's media empire ensured publicity for these polls, as well as intensive coverage for the movement.

As well as controlling interests in a variety of printed media, Fininvest controlled the three national private television networks, Canale 5, Italia 1 and Rete 4. With this help, Berlusconi succeeded in creating what has been dubbed a 'virtual party', devoid of tradition and genuine grass-roots activism. It was, however, a vehicle sufficient to take Berlusconi to power. But even Forza Italia!'s media resources and its image as a fresh force in Italian politics could not have secured victory without electoral cooperation among the main parties of the right in the new single-member constituencies. Under the new electoral rules, the right's electorate would have been split, in the north by the League and in the south by the AN, and the left contender would probably have been allowed through. And so an unlikely and ultimately unstable alliance was put together, based more on pragmatic recognition of the implications of the new electoral rules than on any commitment to common programmatic ends.

In terms of electoral mechanics, the Forza Italia!–AN–Northern League alliance served its purpose. Forza Italia! and its junior partners together secured 46 per cent of the vote. The coalition gained an absolute majority in the Chamber of Deputies, securing more than half the seats, and was the largest grouping in the Senate.

The Berlusconi administration

Following the right's victory in the elections, President Oscar Luigi Scalfaro invited Silvio Berlusconi to form a government. This was an important test for the idea that the new electoral arrangements had ushered in a new era in Italian politics. If the leader of the winning bloc could rely on the unquestioning support of a majority of parliamentarians, he would have a much freer hand to pick the new cabinet. Of course, Prime Ministerial free choice in the selection of the cabinet is largely an ideal even in the UK's traditionally two-party, majoritarian political system, as the allocation of important ministerial posts is often made bearing in mind the need to reward loyal allies and appease potential rivals. In the immeasurably more complex process of cabinet formation in Italy, with its tradition of multiple coalitions and factionalised parties, the process of haggling over the allocation of posts could be very lengthy indeed. In this respect, the new Berlusconi government was no departure from the old patterns of Italian politics. Despite its majority, it took the rivalrous coalition a full six weeks to form a government. One of the main problems for the new leader was the pacification of Umberto Bossi, the charismatic leader of Northern League, who asserted that he would participate only in a government committed to the introduction of federalism at the earliest possible time.

The announcement of Berlusconi's new government finally came on 10 May 1994. The line-up included five ministers from the AN, three of whom had been leaders of the MSI. The success of the former Fascists in gaining representation in the cabinet touched a very sensitive political nerve, both in Italy and more widely in Europe. But the new government rode out the uproar and the neo-Fascist ministers retained their posts. It was an early sign that the new government would be unwilling to make much accommodation with societal pressures. In this sense, the new government did differ from the DC regime, which, at least in its latter years, had often been able to bend to the left without breaking. The new coalition of the right appeared from the outset as an altogether more brittle affair. This would be confirmed later, when the government's uncompromising attitude towards mass protest against its plans to cut spending on pensions was a key factor in its fall.

The majoritarian philosophy of the Berlusconi government

Even before the difficult birth of the new government, Berlusconi and his team of advisers (many of whom were former business associates) were insistent that the 1994 elections marked a real turning point, a major transformation of the mechanics and philosophy of government in Italy. Berlusconi's understanding was that his government, having been elected under the new rules, represented a clear majority that had defeated the opposition. As such, it should be given a free rein to do its job until the time came for the electorate to judge it again. Compromise and concession with forces of opposition, inside or outside government, were unacceptable, as they would fudge this transparent democratic process. Although the 1948 constitution had not been revised, the majoritarian reform of the electoral system, which had resulted from popular pressure, was seen as overriding the system of power-sharing and dispersal foreseen in the constitution and gradually put into operation over the intervening years. In the view of the government and its supporters, Italy's problems resulted from the multitude of independent institutions capable of authoritative criticism of and interference in government, and especially from an over-powerful and ungovernable parliament, in which opposition groups were able to pervert the intentions of the executive. Even before a government elected on a majoritarian basis had actually come into existence, arguments were being made to protect its future rights. When the Ciampi government introduced reforms of the public administration intended to clamp down on corrupt practices, objections were raised that such reforms would constrain the freedom of an incoming, more legitimate government elected according to majoritarian principles.

This interpretation of the special legitimacy and rights of the executive in the Second Republic became a major theme of the Berlusconi administration. It was repeated with such formulaic insistence that it even began to penetrate the language of the left, whose philosophy was underpinned with respect for the consensual constitution it had helped to write. Berlusconi's polemic with the liberal institutions of Italy's constitution assumed a high public profile early in the life of the new administration following an extraordinary exchange of letters between the new Prime Minister and the President of the Republic. Clearly worried by the inclusion in government of neo-Fascist ministers, President Scalfaro expressed his concern that the new government might not feel itself bound by the domestic and international commitments made by previous governments and that disregard for the rights and conditions of minorities might lead to social unrest. Scalfaro's letter counselled Berlusconi to observe the constitutional principles of liberty and legality, to assure fidelity to international alliances, the politics of European unity, and the politics of peace, and to be respectful of social solidarity, with especial regard to the employment needs of youth. Berlusconi's reply could have done little to allay the President's anxieties about the tone and intentions of the new government. The Prime Minister stated that he 'intended to exercise, without reserve, his power and duty to coordinate and guide the executive office'. Scalfaro showed a very active interpretation of his role as independent guarantor of the constitution throughout the short life of the Berlusconi government.

The Berlusconi government and the institutions

Parliament

A first gesture in the new government's radical reinterpretation of the procedures of government came with the election of the presidents of the two houses of parliament. The presidents play an important role in the organisation of the parliamentary agenda and holding a presidency is an asset to the opposition. In Italy's pure bicameral system, an opposition president can ensure that the executive cannot set all the terms of the debate and steamroller legislation through.

With their rapid action to capture both posts for themselves, the governing parties made a highly symbolic departure from normal practice. Since the mid-1970s, it had been customary for the government to assign one of the presidencies, as well as several chairs of parliament's standing committees, to the opposition. The announcement of the chairs of the parliamentary committees in the Chamber of Deputies came as further confirmation of the government's interpretation of its electoral victory. The ruling coalition had again used its majority to ensure none fell to the opposition. However, the opposition parties retaliated shortly after in the Senate. Here, Berlusconi's coalition did not have a majority and many committee chairs were assigned to opposition groups.

The judiciary

The judiciary had been a target of the presidentialist tradition in Italian politics for some time. Bettino Craxi, leader of the PSI, had set a precedent for attacks on the powers of the magistrates in 1981, in the context of the attempted suicide while in prison of Roberto Calvi. Calvi – the P2 banker who later died in mysterious circumstances hanging under Blackfriars Bridge in London (see chapter 7) – had confessed while in prison to channelling illegal finances to the PSI. Following his suicide attempt, Craxi accused the Milanese magistrates who were investigating Calvi's activities of driving the banker to his act of desperation with their 'intimidatory violence'. This theme was to be a strong motif of the Berlusconi government.

In Italy, the judiciary is highly independent from government, at least in a formal sense. Through most of Italy's post-war history this formal independence was masked by the permeation of the institutions of the judiciary, including its governing body, by the parties and factions. Few magistrates were prepared to blight their promotion prospects by upsetting the apple cart. However, independent-minded magistrates could occasionally use their very broad powers effectively, as was shown, for example, in the uncovering of links between secret organisations and elements within the State and establishment, described in the previous chapter. The independence of the magistrates increased as the hold of the traditional parties weakened following the collapse of Communism in

Europe. The revelations from magistrates' enquiries into corruption in 1992–3 were, of course, the immediate cause of the collapse of the DC and PSI, and the election of a new government in 1994, heralded as the beginning of a new era, did not dissuade the judicial activists from their determination to continue the work of rooting out corruption.

The Berlusconi government responded to the continuation of investigations with increasing irritation, especially as they began to focus on Berlusconi's own business empire. Berlusconi had, of course, been elected in large part because of his appeal as a businessman, a political neophyte untainted by the corrupt politics of the old regime of the parties. But judicial enquiries uncovered evidence suggesting that his business empire had not been immune to the virus of corruption affecting the body politic. Whether or not Berlusconi was personally aware of it, persons within his closest business and family circles had acted corruptly, and the Milan-based Clean Hands team of investigating magistrates were intent on unravelling the story of his company's involvement in bribery and corruption. Berlusconi repeatedly attacked the Clean Hands team, characterising them as the 'red robes' – an epithet suggesting they were pawns of the former PCI. The government and its supporters argued that the magistrates were carrying through a politically motivated campaign against Berlusconi while turning a blind eye to illegal financing of the PCI, especially from Moscow.

The government also made capital from arguments that the magistrates were abusing their powers to arrest and detain subjects before trial, using detention as a form of torture to extract concessions. The powers of the magistrates are, in fact, a thorny issue. On the one hand, they have proved effective in the fight against corruption. On the other, they clearly do pose a threat to civil liberties.

Arguments about the political motivations and excessive powers of the magistrates were used to justify a sustained and very public battle against them. In July 1994, the Minister of Justice, Biondi, issued a decree restricting the magistrates' powers to arrest and detain suspects. The Clean Hands team threatened to quit and a major public outcry led to the retraction of the decree. It later emerged that the decree would have helped a number of high-profile Fininvest associates who had recently come under investigation by the magistrates. The investigations involved the head of Fininvest's tax department, and Silvio Berlusconi's younger brother Paolo, both on charges of bribing the Italian tax police.

The battle between the executive and the judiciary was stepped up still further in October 1994. In a highly contentious move, the Minister of Justice ordered a ministerial inspection of the Milan Clean Hands team to assess charges of abuse made by persons implicated in anti-corruption investigations. Given the constitutional independence of the judiciary in Italy, internal disciplinary matters are supposed to be the responsibility of its governing body, the Superior Council of the Judiciary, and not a government ministry. In the event, however, the ministerial inspection absolved the team. In November 1994, Berlusconi was issued with an official warning that he himself was under investigation concerning the bribes paid by Fininvest companies to the tax police, an accusation he continues to deny vehemently.

The battle between the Berlusconi government and the judiciary was not concluded, as Berlusconi resigned the premiership in December 1994. The allegations against him were not the direct cause of his resignation; however, they undoubtedly increased the pressure on him and have somewhat tarnished his appeal.

The media

In modern democracies, the media are conceived as a vital means for the public to scrutinise the activities of governments. In the UK, public sector television is deeply concerned to defend its reputation of independence from government pressure. In Italy, the public sector broadcasting corporation, the RAI, could not boast this sort of independence. In line with general practices in the public sector, the RAI administrative board is appointed by the presidents of the two chambers of parliament and the nominations were traditionally based on party political affiliation. Control over the three channels was divided among the DC, PSI and PCI, with the DC claiming the best-resourced RAI 1.

Berlusconi's mounting preoccupation with the continued power of the opposition in the new era inaugurated by his government led him into conflict with the RAI. According to Berlusconi, the continued influence of the opposition within public sector television was illegitimate. It was an anomaly, he believed, that public sector television should continue to side with those who had been defeated in the general elections (although to others, the prospect of Berlusconi owning most of private sector television and controlling the public sector broadcaster through his domination of government presented a still greater anomaly). But Berlusconi's complaints of bias were not entirely unfounded, as employees in public sector broadcasting felt their interests were threatened by the new government and tended to look to the left for protection. However, once again, there was a sub-theme to the government's quarrel with public sector television: Berlusconi, through his holding company Fininvest, had a near monopoly over private sector television. The RAI was his major rival for television audiences and for the important revenues that come from the sale of advertising slots.

Under the preceding Ciampi government, a non-political board of directors had been appointed by the presidents of Chamber and Senate to loosen the hold of the parties on the RAI and return it to commercial viability. This was a difficult task, as public sector television was notoriously riddled with party appointees used to virtually limitless funding from public money and very little accountability over how it was spent. However, the Ciampi government appointees were making some headway towards renewing personnel on a more meritocratic basis. Worst of all, from Berlusconi's point of view, there were growing signs that the RAI could be revitalised to compete effectively with the private sector. But Ciampi's board had less than a year to try to reform the RAI, before a run-in with the Berlusconi government forced it to resigned in June 1994. A new board, as customary, was appointed by the presidents of the two chambers, who – as noted earlier – were both drawn from the parties of Berlusconi's right-wing alliance. The new five-person RAI board, nominated in July, contained three persons effectively chosen by the government. However, the president of the Chamber of Deputies, Irene Pivetti of the Northern League, made a stand against the government and nominated two independents. Pivetti publicly denounced the pressure she had been put under to select persons agreeable to the government.

In mid-September, the RAI board named new network directors and heads of news departments. There was considerable unease with the frankly political nature of the appointments, many of whom were associated with Fininvest, and/or had links with either Forza Italia! or the AN. The Northern League was particularly outraged, perhaps because Pivetti's independent stance had denied them any appointees of their own. Surrounded by continual political controversy, the pro-government board was not able to make much progress towards silencing the opposition in public sector television. Over the autumn and winter of 1994, a somewhat lower profile was given to social protest and to the Northern League's rebellions against the majority of which it formed part and Berlusconi received generally more favourable coverage. However, some anti-government voices remained in place, especially in RAI 3, which had been the domain of the PCI/PDS since its entry into the spoils-sharing system in public television in the late 1970s.

The conflict-of-interest debate

Another theme that dominated headlines during Berlusconi's premiership was the conflict between his interests as the owner of a vast business empire, whose fortunes could be profoundly affected by the actions of government, and his role as head of government. A characteristic of post-war Italy has been the permeation of the State by societal interests. Private business was often able to 'buy' public contracts or advantageous legislation, for example in return for contributions to party finances. For its critics, Berlusconi's premiership represented the extreme form of this tendency: a virtual fusion of the public and private. What is more, the Prime Minister's business was much in need of political help at the time. By late 1993, Fininvest's debts were estimated at 6,000 billion lire. Unsurprisingly, suspicions were voiced that Berlusconi's entrance into politics was motivated as much by the need to restore an ailing business to health as to rescue Italy from the Communist threat. Berlusconi had received considerable help in building his business from his old friend Bettino Craxi, leader of the PSI and Italy's longest-serving Prime Minister, holding that office between 1983 and 1987. Craxi had been utterly discredited in the corruption scandals of the early 1990s and fled Italy to escape a prison sentence of almost twenty-six years. In the absence of a powerful political patron, it was said, Berlusconi was forced to do the job himself.

Berlusconi made a variety of attempts to resolve the conflict-of-interest question. In January 1994 he turned over his presidency of Fininvest to a friend and close business associate, Fedele Confalonieri. However, this did little to alleviate suspicions, as control of his business would return to him following his term of office, together with any benefits that may have accrued to it through his exercise of power. The same flaw marred other suggestions, such as the setting up of a US-style blind trust. Even his November announcement that he intended to sell all his business holdings did not allay suspicions, in part because the complexity of his business operations would mean that the process of their sale would inevitably be very lengthy and in part because of suggestions that there were anyway good business reasons to sell off at least part of the empire. By the time of Berlusconi's resignation from the premiership, the issue had still not been resolved.

The fall of the Berlusconi government

Berlusconi ran in the electoral campaign on a programme of fighting unemployment, reducing taxes and opening Italy to the forces of the market. But in reality, the major policy objective of the government was the drastic reduction of Italy's gigantic public debt, overblown by decades of public sector expansion, the waste and inefficiency arising from the clientelistic use of public resources and tax revenues diminished by extraordinary levels of tax evasion. A reduction in public sector spending, and especially in the bill footed by the government for pensions, was widely seen as essential if Italy was to achieve early participation in EMU. Unsurprisingly, this strategy put the government on a collision course with the trade unions (an account of Italy's generous pension system and its importance, especially to the most organised sectors of employees, is given on pp. 109–11).

In late September 1994, government proposals for the 1995 budget foresaw a 50,000 billion lire reduction in spending, to be gained from a combination of welfare cuts and a tax amnesty, in which the payment of a nominal sum would absolve tax evaders from past misdemeanour. In response, the trade unions called a general strike, in which more than three million people participated. Berlusconi called for them to get back to work and declared that strikes would not influence the government's economic decisions. On 12 November, more than a million people demonstrated against the budget: it was Italy's largest demonstration since the immediate post-war period. Still Berlusconi was adamant that no accord could be reached with the unions. This stance was not fully supported even within his own majority, as the Northern League was by now publicly accusing the government of deliberately fomenting public unrest. Another general strike was called for 2

December. On the eve of the strike, an accord on pensions was negotiated between the government and the unions and the strike was cancelled.

The defeat of the Berlusconi administration's set-piece legislation after widespread popular dissent fatally undermined the government. On 17 December, the government faced a series of no-confidence motions, one of which was supported by parts of Berlusconi's own majority among the Northern League and the PPI. Berlusconi did not wait for the vote, which was a foregone conclusion. On 22 December, he handed in his resignation to the President of the Republic.

The Dini government

The fall of Berlusconi's government did not result in a general election, but in a period of stewardship by Lamberto Dini, who had been Finance Minister in the Berlusconi administration and was also a former director of the Bank of Italy. Dini's 'technical' or 'non-political' cabinet (which for the first time included no MPs) governed in place of an elected political leadership for fifteen months through 1995 and into 1996. In retrospect, it can be seen as a sort of dress rehearsal for the centre-left, for the majority put in power by the elections of March 1994 had been dissolved and Dini's centre-right, market-oriented administration was kept in office by the previous opposition, led by the PDS, together with elements of the old majority.

Berlusconi and his supporters insistently claimed that democracy had been subverted by the non-electoral overturning of his majority. However, the vociferous and disruptive opposition of the former governing bloc contrasted with the centre-left's support for the technical government, which was intended as a temporary leadership to guide the country through essential reforms during a period of political, institutional and economic difficulty. The centre-left undoubtedly later benefited from the perception that it had acted in a constructive and responsible manner, placing the national interest above partisan concerns.

The main task of Dini's government was to carry through the pension reform that the Berlusconi government had been unable to conclude. On completion of this responsibility it was pledged to resign.

The Dini government's approach to achieving pension reform stood in sharp contrast to that of its predecessor. Although a tough mini-budget was introduced by Dini's cabinet in February 1995, pension reform was achieved through consultation with the trade unions. The reform included a number of concessions to employees. For example, pensions were to be linked to contributions rather than salaries. This closed the way to a common form of abuse by self-employed workers, who were often able to manipulate their declared earnings to show high incomes in the last years of their working lives in order to boost their pensions. In another concession, the reformed rules were to apply only to new employees, so that people who had made their retirement plans on the basis of the old rules were not affected. The reform also included an increased role for private pension schemes and the gradual reduction of State spending on pensions.

Dini's premiership suffered a brief interruption in early 1996, when the government lost its majority. Antonio Maccanico was Prime Minister for two weeks, until 14 February. He was unable to put together a working majority and the premiership returned to Dini. The episode served to underline the pressing need for an elected government that could base its claim for legitimacy on a popular mandate.

The changing balance of political forces and the run-up to the 1996 general election

The left's willingness to support a centre-right, market-oriented government led by a former minister of Berlusconi's right-wing administration almost certainly gave it credit with those sectors of the electorate who were nervous about entrusting government to an alliance dominated by the former Communists. The value of this political capital was first realised in the regional elections of April 1995, when centre-left coalitions won in nine of the fifteen ordinary regions. The left also benefited from its greater unity and, negatively, from the increasingly tarnished image of the right and its leader, who was still beleaguered by allegations about his company's involvement in bribing tax inspectors.

However, the right was by no means a spent force, as was demonstrated by the result of a referendum on television ownership held a few weeks later. The referendum, promoted with the intention of forcing a break-up of Berlusconi's media empire, resulted in a decisive victory for Berlusconi and Forza Italia! The referendum delivered to the right its media outlet. But it could not deliver unity around a clear programme for the future, nor, even more importantly, an organisation firmly rooted within the electorate.

As noted earlier in this chapter, Forza Italia! was really formed to fill a vacuum on the right of politics created by the collapse of the DC. It did not emerge as the expression of needs, interests and perspectives felt by a particular constituency or sector of the population, but was marketed to the electorate rather like a commercial brand is marketed and using similar techniques. Its leadership was drawn, ready made, from Berlusconi's business empire and was not ratified by a national forum such as a party conference. Local party structures were created in the 14,000 or so Forza Italia! clubs, but these were bypassed by the leadership in all important decisions and largely withered away once their immediate electoral function had been fulfilled. The party, in other words, lacked an organisational reality within which to integrate its support and carry its message. Thus in the run-up to the 1996 elections, Forza Italia! was handicapped by its organisational weakness, the allegations of corruption and the loss of the claim to be an entirely fresh force in politics, a claim, of course, that can be used only once. Given the added handicap of the break-up of the right-wing electoral coalition due to the defection of the Northern League, even Berlusconi's continuing media influence could not help the right-wing bloc to repeat the success of 1994.

When the votes had been counted and the seats assigned, it emerged that the Olive Tree alliance, dominated by the PDS, had a majority in both houses of parliament, although in the Chamber of Deputies it needed the support of Communist Refoundation, which was not part of the alliance.

The first government of the left

The outcome of the Italian general election of 21 April 1996 was historic. The old pattern of post-war politics, in which the left was permanently locked out of participation in national government by the fear of Communism, had finally been broken. For the first time, Italy was to have a government dominated by the former Communists and supported by the left-wing breakaway Communist Refoundation. What can account for this seismic change in the nature of Italian politics?

The unblocking of Italian politics had not come out of the blue. Early warning of the impending disaster for the DC-dominated coalition system came in the so-called earthquake election of 1992, when the major parties had suffered damaging losses and the smaller, non-traditional parties made gains at their expense. This was the first general election since the end of the Cold War, to which the demise of the shifting coalitions of the DC is inextricably linked.

Intuitively, the collapse of Communism in Europe should have fatally undermined the PCI by depriving it of a model and aspiration. And in an important sense this did in fact occur, as the PCI took on a new name identifying it clearly as a broadly social democratic party able to cooperate with a wide range of social and political forces. This transformation ultimately facilitated the PDS in its search for new alliances with which to fight elections under the new rules brought in in 1993. In 1994 the left alliance was defeated, but by 1996 it looked more coherent than the temporary coalition of the right that took Berlusconi to power.

In the 1996 election, furthermore, the PDS made the politically astute decision to concede the leadership of its Olive Tree alliance to Romano Prodi, rather than to Massimo D'Alema, its own general secretary. This did much to allay old fears, as the Prime Minister, in the event of a left-wing victory, would not be a former Communist but a university economics professor and former head of the IRI who had had strong links with the DC. The PDS had yet another advantage in the 1996 election that it had never enjoyed before. For the first time it was competing as a responsible partner in power, whose support for the interim Dini government had seen the country through a time of potential crisis.

Interestingly, however, the centre-left majority of the parliamentary seats did not reflect a real swing to the left. Under the proportional part of the system in the election to the Chamber of Deputies, the combined vote of the PDS and Communist Refoundation, at 29.7 per cent, did not quite match the PCI's peak vote of 1976 and was only just over 3 per cent higher than its vote in 1994. The vote for Forza Italia! and AN in 1996 was, at 36.3 per cent, higher than the vote for the left. The main reason why the left emerged as the victor in the 1996 election was the fragmentation of the right and the disadvantage this gave it under the mainly majoritarian electoral system.

In 1994, the Northern League ran in the 'Pole of Good Government', separate from but linked in a pact with the 'Freedom Pole' alliance dominated by Forza Italia! and AN. In 1996, the Northern League ran on its own, draining crucial votes from the Freedom Pole in the north. Further votes were almost certainly taken from the right-wing alliance by Italian Renewal – a new party formed under Dini's leadership, as well as by a far-right grouping that had broken away from the AN–MSI after it dissolved and renamed itself the AN in 1995.

The centre-left was relatively more united. The Olive Tree alliance was made up of or supported by a large number of distinctive components (PDS, Communist Refoundation, PPI, Greens, Segni's Pact for Italy and eleven minor organisations) and there was much potential for conflicts of interest. However, the alliance functioned as an electoral coalition, beating the divided right in a sufficient number of single-member constituencies to take it into power.

The alliance has also proved surprisingly durable in power, although not immune to crisis. The Prodi government relies on the continuing support of Communist Refoundation, which is reluctant to be seen sharing responsibility for spending cuts, especially on pensions.

The tasks of the Prodi government

The first and most momentous task of the centre-left administration led by Prodi has been to reconcile Italy's fragmented political forces to a constitutional reform that all can accept. The importance and complexity of this task have already been described in chapter 2 and have been a recurrent theme of this book. The first stage of this task has already been accomplished, with the preparation by a specially constituted bicameral commission of a draft reform. This reform must now be ratified by parliament and people, a process that is unlikely to be completed before the end of 1998.

The other major task of the Prodi administration has been to continue the efforts of its predecessors to whittle down Italy's public debt and permanently reduce public spending. The approach taken to this thorny problem has by necessity been consensual. Prodi's government has a distinct market orientation, which creates unease within the trade unions and on the left. As well as the massive privatisation programme, which, given the abuse of public resources under the old regime, is not as contested by the left as might be expected, plans include the creation of markets in housing and education.

Little has emerged in the way of a concrete programme to tackle unemployment, apart from recommendations that the rigidity of the labour market should be reduced to allow employees to price themselves into a job. However, radical reforms of the labour market, for example allowing employers a free hand to use temporary workers, were impossible given the opposition to such measures by Communist Refoundation and the trade unions. The unions were assured that concessions enshrined in the landmark central agreement thrashed out in 1993 (see p. 121), including limitations on the use of temporary workers, were to be respected. The approach to welfare reform has also been consensual, the planned reforms being drawn up by a commission of neutral experts.

Prospects for the future

It is too early for an attempt to predict the future shape of Italian politics when governments remain unstable and major constitutional reform is on the way. Nevertheless, the party system and the nature of government have already undergone major transformations under the impact of the collapse of the traditional parties and the new electoral system, and it is possible to make some preliminary comment on these.

The new electoral system in which the PR element has been reduced to 25 per cent has had a decisive impact, most notably in that an alternation of government has occurred. What is more, the electorate now has the chance to include the identity of the future Prime Minister in their calculations and this strengthens the hand of this office. However, the 1993 reforms alone do not guarantee a clear-cut choice between left and right blocs and between two candidates for the premiership. A realignment of the majority, even between elections, remains a possibility. This was first shown in 1995 by the substitution of Lamberto Dini's technical government for the elected Berlusconi government. Dini was able to piece together a new parliamentary majority with the support of the opposition to the Berlusconi government and some elements of the old majority. It was this overturning of the electoral result that so infuriated Berlusconi.

The potential for mid-term mutations of government was illustrated again during the Prodi government, when the PDS appeared to contemplate an alliance with Forza Italia! to free itself from its dependence on Communist Refoundation. However, the political fall-out from such an alliance would probably be costly to both partners.

The reshaping of the party system under pressure of the electoral reform has progressed, although the outcome of two main moderate blocs on the left and right of centre has not been achieved. The centre-left government has shown that a broad alliance of progressive forces is possible in election campaigns and in government. However, D'Alema's project of a big social democratic party that can embrace the constituencies of Catholics, ex-socialists and the old lay parties and thus implicitly marginalise Communist Refoundation is still a long way from realisation. The prospects for a unified national party of the centre-right seem even more uncertain, at least under the current constitutional arrangements. The Northern League and the AN remain at loggerheads and Forza Italia! still suffers from organisational weaknesses.

The problem of fragmentation is not amenable to rapid reform from above. The Italian party system is historically spread over a wide ideological spectrum and parties and their constituencies are unwilling to give up historic identities, traditions and ideologies to subsume themselves into two blocs offering bland ideologies which locate them near the centre of political opinion.

Whatever the future for Italy is, the brief experience of the Berlusconi government indicates that government by a majority to the exclusion of a minority is not workable, not least because a homogeneous majority does not yet exist. Attempts to impose governability by narrowing the potential for opposition, although perhaps tempting in the light of continued government instability, would lead to a loss of democracy while not necessarily solving problems of ingrained corruption.

Further reading

Buffacchi, V. 'The Coming of Age of Italian Democracy', *Government and Opposition*, Vol. 31, No. 3 (1996).
Donovan, M. 'The 1994 Election in Italy: Normalisation or Continuing Exceptionalism?', *West European Politics*, Vol. 17, No. 4 (1994).
Katz, R. S. and Ignazi, P. *Italian Politics: The Year of the Tycoon*, Oxford (1996).

9

Italy in the world

Introduction

The colonial past of the European nations has informed in various ways the patterns of trade, friendship and ambition that underpin their contemporary relations in the world. Colonial possessions brought many advantages to the coloniser. They brought prestige and standing in the international order. They gave access to cheap raw materials, many of which, due to climate or geographical accident, could not be grown or extracted in Europe. They provided growing markets for the finished goods manufactured in the more industrially advanced colonial nation. They offered room to expand – space into which excess population could be drained off.

The conquest of foreign territories also fostered the development of patriotism in the colonial power. Victory in wars of conquest was a source of national pride – even though the sides were not evenly matched, given the vast European advantage in the industrially produced technology of war and in military organisation. The subjugation of other peoples often provided a release for internal tensions. The possession of colonies brought with it an imaginary hierarchy in which all the people of the colonising nation, including the most wretched and potentially rebellious, could congratulate themselves on their own racial and cultural 'superiority'.

The liberal era

Italy's ambitions in Africa

During the main period of Europe's colonial expansion in Africa, Italy was ill-placed to compete. In the UK, France and Germany, the development of industry revolutionised society in the first half of the nineteenth century, giving rise to the search for raw materials, market outlets and investment opportunities abroad. Italy's main period of expansion came later, from the very end of the nineteenth century. When Italy entered the ranks of the major industrialised European nations, Africa had largely been divided up already, the lion's share having gone to the UK and France. But industrialisation had brought with it new needs and ambitions in Italy, too. Italy did not want to be left out of the division of the spoils, or remain an uninfluential player in world affairs.

In the early years of the twentieth century, international negotiations, mainly with France, cleared the way for Italian designs on North Africa. The Italians consented to French penetration of Morocco in return for recognition of Italian influence over the Libyan region. In 1911, on the eve of the Balkan Wars, the other colonial powers rewarded Italy for its compliance by allowing it to take Libya from the Turks. It was an unpopular war in which a mountainous, sandy and poorly irrigated land was acquired at the cost of thousands of lives. Bitter internal opposition to the war by socialists was a major cause of Prime Minister Giovanni Giolitti's concession of an extension of male suffrage in 1912 in a move to restore the government's popularity.

The 1911–12 Libyan war, which pitted Italian troops against irregular Arab troops under Turkish command, also revealed Italy's military weakness: its colonial ambitions were not matched by its material and organisational preparation for military conquest.

Italy's ambitions in Europe

A major influence on Italian foreign policy in the liberal era was the sense that unification was incomplete while territory such as South Tyrol, Trento and Trieste, whose populations included large numbers of Italian speakers, were still under foreign rule (most importantly from Austria). However, Italy also had ambitions to extend its territory and influence beyond the areas where its claims might be justified by linguistic and cultural affinity. Italy also had designs, for example, in the Istrian Peninsula, Dalmatia and Albania.

Territorial ambitions were a major factor in Italy's intervention in the First World War. A great majority in the country and in parliament were opposed to it. For the PSI, the war was an inter-imperial dispute. Italian socialists remained committed to non-intervention, even when their counterparts elsewhere in Europe became converted to the patriotic cause, in which the interests of class were dropped in favour of the national interest of defence against external aggression. Many Liberals feared that Italy was ill-prepared for war in economic and military terms and were worried that intervention would exacerbate social tensions to the point of civil war and revolution (as in fact happened in Russia). Although the Vatican had sympathies for the Catholic Austrian monarchy, and loathed secular and Republican France, the Italian peasantry, who formed its main social basis, were pacifist, as it was from this group that most front-line troops would be drawn. Even most industrialists and financiers were opposed to war, as they expected to make profits from the supply of the materials of war to both sides.

Nevertheless, Italy was dragged into the war mainly through the actions of nationalist interventionists who had great influence in the executive and on the monarchy. In April 1915, Italy committed itself to war with the Treaty of London, which was to remain secret until 1917. In return for intervening on the side of the UK, France and Russia, Italy was promised the Austrian-ruled territories it had long claimed, as well as Slavic territories in Istria and Dalmatia, a protectorate over Albania and the Dodecanese islands off Turkey. Vague promises of further colonial spoils were also made.

The First World War

Italy's intervention in the First World War was for most sectors of society a deeply damaging experience. Although there were some notable victories, the military skills and resources of the Italian troops were for the most part inadequate and there were humiliating defeats, such as the rout of Caporetto in October 1917. In many cases, discipline was maintained only under the harshest repression and desertion was common, even though the punishment was death.

Technically, Italy emerged from the First World War as a victor. But the cost of war had been terrible, perhaps even more so than in countries where the people had been united by a common patriotic spirit and where the mass socialist parties had helped bring working people together in the fight against Central European or Tsarist authoritarianism, depending on perspective. In Italy, where socialist pacifism had been more consistent, the war for most people was experienced as an unjustified suffering imposed by a ruling class that had profited massively from it through speculation. The divisive effects of the war were exacerbated by Italy's meagre gains from it.

At the end of the war, Italy was massively divided internally in a crisis that would be 'resolved' only by the advent of Fascist authoritarianism. In addition, its military contribution to the war had been modest, despite its enormous cost in human and economic terms. As a result, Italy was in a weak position when the victors came to carving up the spoils in negotiations dominated by the US, the UK and France. The promises of the Treaty of London were quietly forgotten by the British and French. The Americans, who had not been a signatory, obviously did not feel bound by it and were anyway profoundly opposed to the practices of European imperialism. President Wilson had no time for Italian pretensions to territories that were not Italian speaking. Although Italy's war resulted in the completion of unification, its aspirations elsewhere were largely frustrated.

The 'mutilated victory' increased the bitterness of nationalist forces in Italy. In September 1919, to the exultation of the nationalists, D'Annunzio led an expedition of rebel troops to occupy the disputed city of Fiume. However, Prime Minister Giolitti had a clearer understanding of the true international balance of power and D'Annunzio was cleared out of Fiume the following January.

Foreign policy under Fascism

Mussolini was determined to leave behind the weaknesses of the liberal era and assert Italy's status as a nation to be feared and respected. In this aim he was initially given some comfort by the British, who favoured the growth of Italian influence, especially in the Balkans, as a counterbalance to the ambitious projects of France in that area.

The aggressive style of Mussolinian foreign policy was exemplified by an attack on the Greek island of Corfu in 1923. In the mid-1930s, Mussolini also returned Italy to an aggressive colonial policy in Africa, most notoriously in the conquest of Abyssinia (Ethiopia). At the time, Ethiopia, under the government of Haile Selassie since 1930, was an independent kingdom, a rarity in Africa after the imperialist scramble of the nineteenth century. Italy had shared neighbouring Somalia with the British since the 1880s, but had become dissatisfied with its barren part of this land and saw independent Ethiopia as a last chance for colonial expansion. Mussolini was determined that Italy, too, should take its 'place in the sun' and add Ethiopia to its existing empire of Libya, Eritrea and Somalia. In October 1935, Italy attacked and by 1936 Italian troops had entered Adis Abeba.

There was considerable consensus in favour of the Ethiopian war within Italy and Mussolini's propaganda promised it would provide 'bread and land' for everyone. The Italian occupation, which saw atrocities such as experimentation with poison gases on the population, was met, however, with international condemnation.

The Second World War brought an end to Italy's colonial exploits in Ethiopia as elsewhere. In April 1941 Adis Abeba was taken by the British, bringing to an end a five-year period of Italian occupation.

The Second World War and the end of the colonial era

On the eve of the Second World War, Italy was still behind the levels of industrialisation achieved by its main European neighbours and had been further weakened by the material and human costs of the Ethiopian war as well as the intervention in favour of General Franco in the Spanish Civil War. Despite this, Mussolini took Italy into war against the Allies, although he waited until the summer of 1940, when France had been defeated and the prospects for German victory seemed strong.

Mussolini's intention was for Italy to wage a separate though parallel war to that of Germany, a war that would have a specifically Italian goal of expansion in the Mediterranean, Africa and the Balkans. However, it was not long before Italy's underlying military weakness was revealed and Mussolini had to be content with a role for Italian Fascism that was almost completely subordinate to that of Nazi Germany. Initially the parallel-war strategy met with some success as Italian troops based in Ethiopia penetrated the Sudan and British Somalia in August 1940. However, Italy suffered later setbacks in Africa as the British forces rallied. In the meantime, the Italian attack on Greece in autumn 1940 was met by a well organised defence. The Greek campaign was a further drain on Italy's overtaxed military resources. By the end of 1940, dreams of the parallel war ended as Germany intervened in Greece and Yugoslavia and German troops came to Italy's aid in North Africa.

The end of the Second World War signalled the beginning of the end for European colonialism. Germany and Italy were deprived of their colonies in the post-war settlements and even the victorious powers were to see their empires gradually eroded in the waves of anti-colonial struggles over the following decades. However, the loss of colonies and spheres of direct influence abroad did not ultimately disadvantage either German or Italian economic development in a world that had emerged reshaped from the second global conflagration. Arguably, the tame markets of the UK's historic empire helped cushion British manufacturers from competition, contributing to its failure to renew ageing technology and update organisational practices and institutional culture.

Germany and Italy, in contrast, were forced to compete unprotected, especially in the giant free market emerging in Europe. Germany emerged as Europe's foremost economic power, but Italy's performance through the economic miracle of the 1950s was no less remarkable given its relatively backward starting-point as a nation that was still predominantly agricultural.

Italy and the USA

Italy's emergence as a major Western industrial power owed much to the USA. However, the debt was, in the end, more political than economic. US economic aid, principally in the form of Marshall Aid, was undoubtedly important in Italy as it was elsewhere in Western Europe, but it was never a major proportion of gross domestic product over the years of its operation. The main role of the USA was to keep its most faithful ally firmly in the Western sphere by ensuring that the PCI was permanently locked out of power.

In June 1945, the acting US Secretary of State wrote: 'Our objective is to strengthen Italy economically and politically so that truly democratic elements of the country can withstand the forces that threaten to sweep them into a new totalitarianism' (Warner, 1972, p. 47). This objective was realised through an unprecedented US intervention in the internal affairs of a European country. The geographical location of

Italy, with its potential for domination of the Mediterranean and its north-eastern border with Tito's Yugoslavia made it extremely sensitive in the Cold War context of post-war Europe. The possibility that a relatively advanced nation of such strategic importance could fall under the influence of Moscow – and perhaps bring other Western countries with it – was a terrifying prospect for the USA. And in the immediate aftermath of the Second World War, the possibility that the Communists could come to power seemed real.

Italy had Europe's largest Communist party outside of the areas dominated by the Soviet Union. The PCI, aided by the prestige it had gained during the Resistance and by important help from the Soviet Union, was on the point of overtaking the PSI as the major party of working people. After its emergence from suppression under Fascism, the PCI grew rapidly to a membership of more than two million. What is more, much of the PSI sympathised with the PCI and the two parties maintained a close relationship until 1956.

From a socio-economic point of view, Italy appeared as a favourable terrain for the spread of Communist ideas. Because of the inadequacy of agrarian reforms, there was no significant class of prosperous farmers whose commitment to private property would pit them against Communism, and in parts of the south a great insurrectionary movement was building, with peasants occupying and working the uncultivated lands of the great estates. In some towns, short-lived 'red republics' were even established, with citizens mining the access roads and setting up people's courts to dispense justice.

In the north, the possibility of Communist insurrection was more remote. Here, the leadership of the PCI was much more entrenched and the Party had explicitly renounced insurrection and committed itself to building socialism through parliament and the gradual transformation of the country's social and economic fabric. For a period, however, the possibility of such a major transformation, using constituted political authority, seemed real. As Nazism and Fascism were forced into retreat with the important help of the Resistance movement, the PCI was collaborating with the other major anti-Fascist forces in the committees of national liberation that had formed a sort of provisional government before central authority, initially on the basis of the old monarchical form, was restored from the south. From April 1945, management councils were established and through these workers were collaborating in the technical management of capitalism.

As central government was restored, both the PCI and PSI were briefly part of the anti-Fascist coalition that ruled Italy. Thus anti-Fascist forces committed to a major social transformation that would threaten the free operation of markets were an important presence in Italy and this, combined with the precedent of Communist and Socialist participation in power, meant that the Italian left constituted a terrible challenge to the world view of the mighty USA. The USA persistently urged Alcide De Gasperi, who became Prime Minister in December 1945, to drop the left from the anti-Fascist coalition government. This he did in summer 1947. De Gasperi's confidence in his manoeuvres against the left was bolstered by a visit to the USA in January 1947 during which he was able to secure a substantial loan.

Intervention by the USA in Italy's internal affairs reached a climax during the campaign leading to the general election of 1948. US aid to Italy received massive publicity. Every one-hundredth ship bearing its cargo of food, medicines and essential supplies from the USA was greeted with great celebration. Hollywood stars recorded messages of support for the DC and the Italo-American community in the USA organised a mass letter-writing campaign to convince family and friends back home to give their vote against Communism.

The carrot was used abundantly in the form of aid, loans and, importantly, the promise, one month before the election, of the return to Italy of part of Trieste that had been under UK and US military occupation. But there was also the stick. As the election neared, US warships were anchored in major Italian ports. In a more sinister move, the USA gave financial and military assistance to clandestine anti-Communist groups and plans were laid for a military occupation of Sicily and Sardinia.

The US intervention in favour of the DC, as the only non-socialist mass party in Italy, continued through the 1950s, exemplified by the attitudes of the US ambassador, Clare Boothe Luce, who went so far as to intervene in the management of private industry, for example admonishing the managing director of Italy's automobile giant FIAT to reduce the strength of the Communist and Socialist trade union in the committees of worker representation.

The USA's hostility to the Italian left did not diminish until the early 1960s. Fearing that continued hostility to the Socialists would drive them into the arms of the Communists, the USA, under President Kennedy, encouraged the opening to the left and the inclusion of the PSI in government from 1962–3.

The end of the Cold War, the fall of the DC dynasty and, since 1996, the establishment of a government of the centre-left have not altered Italy's friendly intent to the giant across the Atlantic. And for the USA, Italy has, if anything, become even more important, as the collapse of the Soviet Union and its satellites has shifted the frontier of anxiety from the centre of Europe to the south.

Italy in Europe after the war

The Second World War had been an enormous blow to the global powers of the great European nations and the USA and the Soviet Union had now emerged as the dominant players in the new international order. With this new order came a new approach to international relations.

The nature of this new approach had first been suggested with the USA's intervention in the First World War. President Woodrow Wilson was profoundly opposed to the policies of the old Europe involving the acquisition of spheres of influence and the imposition of administrative and political control by one nation over another. This sentiment was echoed in the Atlantic Charter of the Second World War. As well as signalling the West's readiness to intervene against the threat of Communist take-over, the Atlantic Charter also confirmed the rights of peoples to their own democratically elected government and to national self-determination.

Italy's attempts to impose itself on the world by force were not ultimately successful. But as post-Fascist Italy dropped its pretensions to be a nation that was feared and respected, its strong suit of diplomacy came to the fore. Italy's capacity to get a large part of what it wanted through able negotiation, the construction of complex trade-offs and package deals is nowhere better demonstrated than in its participation within the European Community, of which it was a founding member.

The economic benefits of Europe to Italy

There are many reasons why Italy was an early and enthusiastic member of the European Economic Community. An early and sustained economic benefit that Italy drew from membership was aid, especially for the chronically underdeveloped south. Of all the current members of the European Union, Italy has enjoyed the largest capital transfers from it.

Membership also helped Italy to deal with its problems of overpopulation and unemployment, especially important given its lack of colonies. The opening of the European borders allowed thousands of Italian workers to seek work in industries outside Italy, most notably in the German car industry. By the 1980s, 1.7 million Italians were resident in other European Community countries.

But probably most important of all, Italy has benefited tremendously from the dismantling of tariff barriers and the opening of European markets to its goods. Unlike the UK, Italy did not have access to big markets in colonies and former colonies. British allegiance to the Commonwealth, and to reciprocally beneficial economic arrangements within it, were an important factor in British reticence towards the European Economic Community. But Italy and Germany, which also lacked a colonial sphere, were able to use the freeing markets of the post-war era, and especially those of Europe, for economic growth based on exports. The Italian economic miracle was founded on the sale abroad of products manufactured by a low-wage labour force. The cheap Italian products were a great success on the European markets and in the first ten years of the Community's existence, Italy's trade with the other member countries rose by 500 per cent.

Political consensus on the benefits of Europe

Membership of the Community brought political as well as economic benefit. The DC leadership sought protection and comfort in close relations with the anti-Communist leaderships of the main West European countries. The left was traditionally more uneasy, tending to see the Community, in common with other European lefts, as a mere capitalist club designed to strengthen the hand of the big capitalist corporations in their search for free markets. However, the broad, cross-party pro-European consensus that now characterises Italy was largely completed by 1970, when the PCI accepted Italy's membership. Even Communist Refoundation do not want Italy to leave the European Union, although they are deeply opposed to any attempts to cut social spending to bring Italy in line with the public debt and spending criteria agreed at Maastricht for entry into EMU.

The only major exception to the political consensus on the benefits of participation in the European project has been on the right. But nationalist sentiments have been a real threat to Italian policy in Europe only once, during the brief Berlusconi administration, in which the former Fascists participated. In this government, the economically hawkish Foreign Minister (a member of Berlusconi's Forza Italia!) emphasised his opposition to the increasing power of the Brussels-based European Union bureaucracy and for a while the possibility of a British–Italian axis of opposition to integration opened up. However, Berlusconi himself remained a supporter of integration.

Popular enthusiasm for Europe

If support for European integration among the political and economic elites and among the political parties has generally been high, this also seems to reflect popular sentiment. Opinion surveys, such as the Union's own Eurobarometer, show consistently high levels of support for the institutions of the European Union. In part, this may reflect a pacifist and anti-nationalist strand of thinking that was reinforced by the experience of Fascism and the idealism of the Resistance movement. Pro-Europeanism may also benefit from a relatively weak concern about issues of national sovereignty in a country that for so long lacked a distinctive foreign policy, being tied to a position of more or less automatic support for the policies of its most powerful allies, especially the USA.

The Italian enthusiasm for political integration

Generally, Italy has been among the most pro-European of the Community member States, its enthusiasm often extending beyond the potential economic benefits the wider markets could bring to Italian capitalism. Currents of thought favouring political union in a federal system of Europe have always been strong in Italy. The Italian Altiero Spinelli, a leading light of the federalist movement of the early years of the Community, dreamed of a political union that would establish a permanent state of peace and harmony in Europe. Alcide De Gasperi, who dominated Italian politics in the early post-war period and was Prime Minister between 1945 and 1953, was

strongly influenced by Spinelli's thought. During the attempts
to build a European defence community in the early 1950s
(attempts which ultimately failed), De Gasperi pressed for the
addition of a political community.

Italy's voice in Europe

Despite the generalised enthusiasm for European integration,
Italy has not had a highly visible role in the shaping of the
European Union and the Communities that preceded it. On the
whole, Italy's role has been as a facilitator, brokering compromises with the more recalcitrant members, and is not
comparable to the high profile of the Franco-German axis. For
example, Italy's neighbours were able to shape the nature of
the Common Agricultural Policy in a way that favoured farmers
of the temperate north rather than those of the Mediterranean
south. The frequent weakness of the Italian voice is largely
explained by the nature of domestic Italian politics.

An important factor in Italy's failure to develop a coherent
voice within Europe is cabinet instability, as post-war governments in Italy have lasted an average of less than ten months.
The recurrent government crises are usually resolved by what
is effectively a cabinet reshuffle, in which ministers are re-
deployed to satisfy the interests and ambitions of party
notables. Thus Foreign Ministers rarely have the opportunity
to master an issue fully, or to establish long-term relations of
mutual understanding with their opposite numbers in the
other member States.

Another problem has been that Italian ministers have often
appeared ill-prepared for meetings of the European Council of
Ministers, the key decision-making institution of the European
Union. The permanent delegation to the Council has com-
plained that Italian ministers are often not fully briefed on the
positions they are supposed to defend, or even that the Italian
officials participating in negotiations have different and even
conflicting positions.

The difficulties in achieving a clear, united and reliable voice in negotiations are further exacerbated by the processes by which Italian policy towards Europe is formed, in which there are no systematic mechanisms for consultation and agreement on a position among the various bodies that will be affected. What is more, negotiating partners cannot be sure that Italian governments will be able to deliver on any promises they make. The institutions of Italian decision-making, described in chapter 2, are complex, fragmented and subject to numerous checks and balances. The executive is weak in relation to parliament and the passage of legislation necessary for the implementation of European policy could not be guaranteed.

Italy's lack of decisive formative impact, combined with its generally staunch support for further integration, have led to perceptions of Italy as a 'yes man' to decisions essentially taken within the more formidable Franco-German axis. The Italian vote can almost always be relied upon in support of the projects of its more proactive partners. But because of this generally supportive attitude, Italy has benefited from benevolent attitudes towards its needs and requests.

As the European Union grows, increasing the number of countries voting in the Council of Ministers, and as a majority, rather than unanimity, is increasingly sufficient for the passage of decisions, Italy's almost automatic support for German and French initiatives will become less necessary. This will increase the pressure on Italy to take an active role in steering policy in the preferred direction, rather than passively accepting the benevolence of 'senior' partners.

Italian influence in the process of integration

But even in the past, Italy's role in European integration and policies has not been as passive as the above account might suggest. An example is the role played by Emilio Colombo in the Italo-German plan to reform procedures known as the

Genscher–Colombo proposals. The proposals, launched at a Community summit meeting of 1981, included the establishment of a comprehensive political and legal framework for the Community as the foundation for further integration. Especially important was the plan to reduce the scope of member States to block Community decisions by invoking vital interests.

The final version of the text (the solemn Declaration of Stuttgart of 1983) was watered down and lacked decisive impact. However, Italian influence in favour of closer integration was again discernible at the Milan summit of 1985. At this meeting, the Italian presidency was able to force through a proposal for an inter-governmental conference to review decision-making procedures, against the opposition of the UK government, headed at that time by Margaret Thatcher. The resulting conference saw the genesis of the Single European Act, in force since 1987. The Act greatly expanded the scope of majority voting in the Council of Ministers, reducing the capacity of individual governments to block developments in the Community. It also enhanced the role of the European parliament and broadened the policy scope of the Community to include areas such as the environment and social policies.

Italy has also been influential in the development of EMU. Commitment to a monetary policy devised at a European level is seen by many Italians as an important external source of discipline to counter the internal competition for public resources that has tended to push public spending ever upwards. The Italian Tomasso Padoa Schioppa was in fact an important author of the criteria for entrance to EMU and is one of the architects of the single currency.

Italy and EMU

Like governments before it, the centre-left administration of Romano Prodi has used the Maastricht criteria to push through spending cuts that will have consequences for pension and welfare spending. The programme of cuts put the relationship between the government and Communist Refoundation (on whose parliamentary votes the government relied) under increasing strain. Communist Refoundation secured a number of concessions that tended to mitigate the cuts, including promises, agreed with the socialist Prime Minister of France, Lionel Jospin, of a major cut in the working week to be funded in part by the State.

Italy's record as a Community member

At least until the early 1990s, Italy had a poor record in the implementation of policy coming from the Community. Italy was one of the worst offenders in terms of failing to translate European directives into national law and had an unwanted record for infringement proceedings started against it. This in part relates to Italian parliamentary procedures noted in earlier chapters: laws have to be passed through the two houses and can be amended, differently, in both and the executive has no special reserve powers to force a bill through.

Recently, however, Italy's record on the translation of Community law has greatly improved. This has much to do with a 1989 Act which introduced an annual Community law, in which a package of directives whose deadlines for implementation are coming up are passed *en bloc*. The timetabling of an annual space in parliament for the passage of Community law has considerably speeded up this aspect of compliance, despite frequent slippage of the date due to unforeseen events such as general elections. However, this new alacrity has not much reduced the number of infringement proceedings against Italy, as the application of the law is still frequently incorrect.

Another area in which Italian performance has been poor is in the uptake of funds assigned by the European Union. The main reason for this has been that Union money comes subject to very stringent rules concerning its use. Money from Rome comes with fewer strings attached and has hence been preferred by spending agencies such as the regions. Italy has been top of the league so far as fraudulent use of European funding is concerned.

Conclusion

The future independence and coherence of the Italian voice in Europe and the world will depend much on the outcome of the major changes currently under way. Italy is a major industrialised nation, both in European and in global terms. It is currently the fifth-ranking nation in terms of gross national product and is a member of the Group of Seven wealthiest industrial nations. A greater stability and democratic legitimacy of Italian governments could enhance its influence, especially in the less predictable post-Cold War world.

Further reading

Warner, G. 'Italy and the Powers, 1943–1949', in Woolf, S. J. (ed.), *The Rebirth of Italy 1943–1950*, London (1972).

Appendix 1

Post-war Prime Ministers and governing coalitions

The table overleaf shows the post-war Prime Ministers (Presidents of the Council of Ministers) and governing coalitions until the crisis in the party system. In June 1992, Giuliano Amato (PSI) formed a new government. By this point, the collapse of the post-war party system was under way and the old coalition 'formulas' had lost their meaning.

Abbreviations used in the table: DC, Democrazia Cristiana (Christian Democracy); PCI, Partito Comunista Italiano (Italian Communist Party); PDL, Partito Democrazia Lavoratori (Democratic Labour Party); PLI, Partito Liberale Italiano (Italian Liberal Party); PPI, Partito Popolare Italiano (Italian Popular Party); PRI, Partito Repubblicano Italiano (Italian Republican Party); PSDI, Partito Socialista Democratico Italiano (Italian Social Democrat Party); PSI, Partito Socialista Italiano (Italian Socialist Party).

Prime Minister	Coalition	Start	End
Ferruccio Parri	DC–PCI–PSI–PLI–PDL–Action Party	June 1945	December 1945
Alcide De Gasperi	DC–PCI–PSI–PLI–PDL–Action Party	December 1945	July 1946
Alcide De Gasperi	DC–PCI–PSI–PLI–PDL–Action Party	July 1946	February 1947
Alcide De Gasperi	DC–PCI–PSI–PRI	February 1947	May 1947
Alcide De Gasperi	DC–PCI–PSI	May 1947	May 1948
Alcide De Gasperi	DC–PLI–PSDI–PRI	May 1948	January 1950
Alcide De Gasperi	DC–PLI–PSDI–PRI	January 1950	July 1951
Alcide De Gasperi	DC–PSDI–PRI	July 1951	July 1953
Alcide De Gasperi	DC–PRI	July 1953	August 1953
Giuseppe Pella	DC	August 1953	January 1954
Amintore Fanfani	DC	January 1954	February 1954
Mario Scelba	DC–PSDI–PLI	February 1954	July 1955
Antonio Segni	DC–PSDI–PLI	July 1955	May 1957
Adone Zoli	DC	May 1957	July 1958
Amintore Fanfani	DC–PSDI	July 1958	February 1959
Antonio Segni	DC	February 1959	March 1960
Fernando Tambroni	DC	March 1960	July 1960
Amintore Fanfani	DC	July 1960	February 1962
Amintore Fanfani	DC–PSDI–PRI	February 1962	June 1963
Giovanni Leone	DC	June 1963	December 1963
Aldo Moro	DC–PSI–PSDI–PRI	December 1963	July 1964
Aldo Moro	DC–PSI–PSDI–PRI	July 1964	February 1966
Aldo Moro	DC–PSI–PSDI–PRI	February 1966	June 1968
Giovanni Leone	DC	June 1968	December 1968

Mariano Rumor	DC–PSI–PRI	December 1968	August 1969
Mariano Rumor	DC	August 1969	March 1970
Mariano Rumor	DC–PSI–PSDI–PRI	March 1970	August 1970
Emilio Colombo	DC–PSI–PSDI–PRI	August 1970	February 1972
Giulio Andreotti	DC	February 1972	June 1972
Giulio Andreotti	DC–PSDI–PLI	June 1972	July 1973
Mariano Rumor	DC–PSI–PSDI–PRI	July 1973	March 1974
Mariano Rumor	DC–PSI–PSDI	March 1974	November 1974
Aldo Moro	DC–PRI	November 1974	February 1976
Aldo Moro	DC	February 1976	July 1976
Giulio Andreotti	DC	July 1976	March 1978
Giulio Andreotti	DC	March 1978	January 1979
Giulio Andreotti	DC–PSDI–PRI	January 1979	August 1979
Francesco Cossiga	DC–PSDI–PLI	August 1979	March 1980
Francesco Cossiga	DC–PSI–PRI	March 1980	September 1980
Arnaldo Forlani	DC–PSI–PSDI–PRI	September 1980	July 1981
Giovanni Spadolini	DC–PSI–PSDI–PRI–PLI	July 1981	August 1982
Giovanni Spadolini	DC–PSI–PSDI–PRI–PLI	August 1982	December 1982
Amintore Fanfani	DC–PSI–PSDI–PLI	December 1982	August 1983
Bettino Craxi	DC–PSI–PSDI–PRI–PLI	August 1983	August 1986
Bettino Craxi	DC–PSI–PSDI–PRI–PLI	August 1986	April 1987
Amintore Fanfani	DC	April 1987	July 1987
Giovanni Goria	DC–PSI–PSDI–PRI–PLI	July 1987	April 1988
Ciriaco De Mita	DC–PSI–PSDI–PRI–PLI	April 1988	August 1989
Giulio Andreotti	DC–PSI–PSDI–PRI–PLI	August 1989	April 1991
Giulio Andreotti	DC–PSI–PSDI–PLI	April 1991	June 1992

Appendix 2
The collapse of the old regime: a chronology

1983

Both the DC and the PCI experience important losses in the general elections. A new regional party, the Liga Veneta, emerges in the north and gets 4 per cent of the vote in the Veneto region.

1987

General elections see an increased vote to the Liga Veneta and the electoral debut of the Lombard League (later to become the Northern League).

8 November 'Yes' votes in a series of referendums give further evidence of public dissatisfaction with politicians and the judiciary.

1989

The fall of the Berlin Wall heralds the end of East European Communism. The leader of the PCI, Achille Occhetto, proposes a change of name for the Party.

1991

February Founding conference of the PDS, formed from the PCI. Part of the left within the former PCI splits to establish Communist Refoundation.

9 June Referendum abolishes the preference vote in elections to the Chamber of Deputies.

1992

17 February Mario Chiesa (PSI), director of a Milan nursing home, is the first of the *'tangentopoli'* (kickback city) arrests.

5–6 April In the general elections, the DC vote drops sharply in the north, although largely holds in the south. The DC reformer Mario Segni gets a high personal vote. The Northern League gets 8–7 per cent nationally, giving it fifty-five MPs.

2 May It is revealed that the mayor and a former mayor of Milan, both PSI functionaries, are under investigation. Bettino Craxi removes his son from the office of secretary of the PSI in Milan.

June Giuliano Amato (PSI) forms a new government.

September and December Local elections in some important councils confirm the electoral decline of the DC and PSI.

10 October Mario Segni leaves the DC.

15 December It is revealed that Craxi is under investigation.

1993

February Craxi resigns as secretary of the PSI. The leader of the Republican Party resigns following notice he is under investigation for illegal party financing.

February–March Five government ministers resign following investigation for corruption.

March The leaders of the Liberal and Social Democrat Parties resign.

18–19 April A series of referendums is held. The most prominent of these leads to the partial abolition of PR in elections to the Senate and make more general electoral reform inevitable. The Amato government resigns immediately after the referendums. Carlo Azeglio Ciampi forms a technical government of non-politicians to lead the country through electoral reform and the annual budget law.

June Local elections see the collapse of the vote for the DC.

June–July The DC dissolves, the mainstream to refound itself as the PPI, a reference to Don Sturzo's original Catholic party.

August Parliament approves new electoral rules under which three-quarters of MPs would be elected on a first-past-the-post basis.

September Umberto Bossi, the leader of the Northern League, threatens the withdrawal of the League's MPs and the establishment of a Northern Republic if general elections are not called by March.

October Craxi starts to cooperate with the magistrates, revealing apparently illicit practices by the PDS.

21 November/5 December In two-round local elections according to new first-past-the-post rules, left-wing mayors are elected in important cities including Rome, Naples, Venice and Genoa. In Palermo, Leoluca Orlando, the leader of the anti-Mafia party, La Rete, is the outright winner at the first ballot.

Bibliography

The following general texts are particularly useful to the student of Italian politics.

Farneti, P. *The Italian Party System (1945–1980)*, London (1985) – a clear introduction to the workings of the Italian party system before its collapse in the early 1990s.

Furlong, P. *Modern Italy: Representation and Reform*, London and New York (1994) – particularly valuable for policy-making processes.

Ginsborg, P. *A History of Contemporary Italy: Society and Politics 1943–1988*, London (1990) – the classic history of the period.

Hellman, S. 'Italy', in M. Kesselman and J. Krieger (eds), *European Politics in Transition*, Lexington, Massachusetts, and Toronto (1987) – very good as a short introduction.

Hine, D. *Governing Italy: The Politics of Bargained Pluralism*, Oxford (1993) – excellent for the constitutional order and generally for the negotiated nature of Italian politics.

La Palombara, J. *Democracy, Italian Style*, New Haven (1987) – an insight into the peculiar nature of democracy in Italy.

Sassoon, D. *Contemporary Italy: Politics, Economy and Society since 1945*, London and New York (1991) – the classic political economy of Italy.

Spotts, F. and Weiser, T. *Italy: A Difficult Democracy*, Cambridge (1986) – very good on the culture of party collusion; includes a chapter on dangers to the State.

See also the yearly series *Italian Politics: A Review*, London.

Index